D1526089

Television Series Regulars
of the Fifties and Sixties
in Interview

"*Everybody has something to say.
It's nice to know that you've
made a difference somewhere.*"
—Dawn Wells—

To my loving husband Carl . . .
Without his love and encouragement, this book
would not have been possible.

And to the memory of my grandmother, Eileen Neal,
a lovely lady who adored writing.

Television Series Regulars of the Fifties and Sixties in Interview

by
Dina-Marie Kulzer

McFarland & Company, Inc., Publishers
Jefferson, North Carolina, and London

Television stills and cast shots are from the author's collection except where noted. Recent portrait photographs were provided by the actors themselves except where noted below. Gary Owens and *Laugh-In* photographs provided courtesy of Gary Owens. Kasey Rogers photographs provided courtesy of Kasey Rogers. Barbara Eden's recent photograph provided courtesy of Hanson and Schwam Public Relations. Connie Stevens' recent photograph provided courtesy of Rogers and Cowan Public Relations. Deborah Walley's recent photograph is by Harry Langdon, and provided courtesy of Deborah Walley. The cast shot from *The Donna Reed Show* is from Columbia Pictures Television.

British Library Cataloguing-in-Publication data are available

Library of Congress Cataloguing-in-Publication Data

Kulzer, Dina-Marie, 1961–
    Television series regulars of the fifties and sixties in interview
/by Dina-Marie Kulzer.
        p. cm.
    Includes bibliographical references and index. ∞
    ISBN 0-89950-722-0 (lib. bdg. : 50# alk. paper)
    1. Television serials—United States—History. 2. Television
actors and actresses—United States—Interviews. I. Title.
II. Title: Television series regulars of the 50s and 60s.
PN1992.8.S4K84 1992
791.45′028′092273—dc20   91-51229
                                                            CIP

Manufactured in the United States of America

McFarland & Company, Inc., Publishers
 Box 611, Jefferson, North Carolina 28640

Contents

v

Acknowledgments

My heartfelt thanks to all of the wonderful actors who graciously spent time discussing their careers and lives with me—I enjoyed every minute of it; to the networks and production companies that produced the series of the fifties and sixties; to Kasey Rogers for her enthusiastic and caring support; to agent Dott Burns for her insight and for putting me in touch with a couple of very important contacts; to my friend and colleague, artist Richard Bartoletti for his help; to my husband Carl for his immense patience and sharp proofreading skills; and to my parents, Victor and Sharon Di Mambro ... for everything.

Introduction

While earlier generations used to have to go to the movie theater each week to see their favorite actors, a child of the "Baby Boom" had a more personal connection to the stars he identified with or even idolized — they came to him in the comfort and security of his own living room every week on television.

There's no question that Baby Boomers spent a good portion of their formative years in front of the television. Devoutly, they followed the characters on series such as *The Adventures of Ozzie and Harriet, Father Knows Best, Family Affair* and *My Three Sons*. Coming into the homes of their audience as they did, the actors on these series brought a very special kind of joy and laughter into the lives of their viewers. Fans and TV characters grew up together.

The voices and faces of those characters are deeply etched into the memories of a generation. When former fans now watch the reruns, it's like flipping back the pages of a family photo album, except this one large family all Baby Boomers have in common.

It could be a rainy Saturday afternoon and there's nothing much going on. Perhaps you're home sick, or a minor case of insomnia has left you sitting in front of the television. Switch through the channels and you can't help running across the flickering, black-and-white or faded color images of your TV family members. You'll find them on the air at just about any time of the night or day, thanks to cable television . . . and, amazingly, they haven't changed a bit.

They say you can't go home again, but by tuning in to these vintage shows you get about as close as you can to recapturing moments and feelings from the past. A TV memory sets off a real life recollection, just as listening to an old song often triggers a memory of where you were the first time you heard it.

Different nights of the week can be associated with various programs from television's golden age. Depending on which decade you recall the best, Monday evenings may be forever linked with *I Love Lucy;* Tuesdays with *The Milton Berle Show;* Thursdays with *Bewitched;* Saturdays with *The Honeymooners,* and Sundays with *The Jack Benny Show.*

Sometimes the theme songs alone will flood you with memories of TV moms who wore impeccable, starched dresses and did housework in

1

high-heel pumps and pearl necklaces; fathers who knew best, understood all, and *always* said the right thing; teenagers who were concerned only with dates, the malt shop and new cars; and wisecracking little brothers or sisters with nothing more to worry about than getting caught in a little white lie or maybe bringing home a bad grade. And don't forget the mischief caused by various TV witches, ghosts, Martians and genies.

Will Sheriff Andy find out that Opie and his friends pushed his police car in front of the fire hydrant? Who will find little Beaver Cleaver trapped inside a steaming soup bowl on top of a huge billboard where he climbed on a dare? Will daddy Danny Thomas figure out that his kids are involved in a conspiracy to pit one parent against the other for the rewards of new toys or allowance raises? Will Ralph Kramden and Ed Norton really strike it rich this time? Will David find out that Ricky is taking his girlfriend to the prom before Ricky can tell him himself? Everyone knows the answers to these all-important questions, but it's still fun and more than just a little comforting to watch.

Right now, I'd like to welcome you to a very special family reunion, contained within the pages of this book. *Television Series Regulars* is a friendly visit with those most remembered from the past. Exclusive interviews reveal who inspired them, what they did before their hit programs, how they felt while they were on the air and what they're doing now. Many also share their film, Broadway and even personal triumphs in addition to their perspective on television. I hope you enjoy your Television Family Reunion...

Ralph Bellamy

Series: Man Against Crime
Role: Mike Barnett (1949–1954)
Series: Frontier Justice
Role: Host (1961)
Series: The Eleventh Hour
Role: Dr. L. Richard Starke (1963–1964)
Series: The Survivors
Role: Baylor Carlyle (1969–1970)

A distinguished actor, with deep-set blue eyes, strong features and a distinctive, resonant voice, Ralph Bellamy played every type of role imaginable in his long, varied career. Many know him for his light comedic roles in the screwball comedies of the thirties; others will remember his awe-inspiring performance as Franklin Delano Roosevelt in *Sunrise at Campobello* both on Broadway and on film. Bellamy was also around at the very inception of television. He was the medium's first detective — one that didn't carry a gun — on the live action series *Man Against Crime*, for which he won the very first Emmy Award as Best Actor.

He began his illustrious career as a teenager "when the smoke hit the fan" (the title of his 1979 autobiography).

"We weren't allowed to smoke on campus in high school, and I smoked. One dismal, fall, overcast, chilly Midwest day after lunch, I wanted a cigarette," elaborated Bellamy in our interview, which took place a few months before his death. "As president of the dramatic club, I had a key to the auditorium. So I went over to the auditorium, let myself in, and went down to the basement. And from a long corridor was coming a pleasant warm draft, which I followed, and at the end of it on the right hand side was a room with a window up at ground level. There was also an enormous wheel about ten feet in diameter, rotating very rapidly, encased in a protective openwork metal device. I lit a cigarette and blew a puff in. I thought it would disappear, which it didn't. It was pared away. It fascinated me. I blew another puff, and presently standing in the doorway was the professor who had caught me at everything I'd done during

3

the last four years. This was just before graduation. And he said, 'What are you doing, Ralph?' And I said, 'Smoking a cigarette.' And he said, 'You know the rules. Will you go over and tell the principal or shall I?' And I said, 'I'll go over.' And I went up through the auditorium and it reeked of cigarette smoke. It was the ventilator that I was blowing the smoke into!" laughs Bellamy. "The principal said, 'This is one too many, you better take your books and go home.' I was kicked out of school. My parents were, of course, upset about that.

"A couple of weeks later, I got a job in a Chatauqua one-night-stand company, under a tent through the middle west," continues the Chicago-born actor. "That was my first job as an actor. From there I went to stock companies in Madison, Wisconsin, Fort Wayne and Evansville, Indiana . . . all through the middle west where you'd stay for ten, twelve or fifteen weeks or more and do a different play every week. You're rehearsing one play all day long, while you're playing in another play at night. And then I went east, did some work in stock and came back and had my own stock company in Des Moines, Iowa, very successfully for two and a half years. I moved to Nashville, Tennessee, and had a year there with my own stock company.

"And from there I went to New York," he laughed, "hoping to get a starring part on Broadway. The first thing that happened is that I went broke. I lived on a bowl of thick heavy soup and quarter loaf of rye bread each day. You could get that meal for fifteen cents in those days — but it was sufficient.

"Then after a while I got an offer from every picture company out here in Hollywood. I came out under contract for Joe Schenck. I never worked for him. He let me out for a couple of pictures. I then went under contract to Harry Cohn at Columbia, and that's a book in itself."

Was the transition from stage to film difficult for Bellamy?

"No, even though it was a different technique I seemed to fit into it. On the stage you're projecting. It's like meeting a new person. Each audience has a personality, they're different, there are no two alike," he explained. "In pictures, you just play the part. And it's a very natural sort of technique. You're not playing to anybody. You're just playing the part . . . portraying the character. I don't go along with method acting. To me, that's not acting. Acting is portraying another character, not being it. Not that there aren't some wonderful method actors. To me the business of acting is going out . . . giving out, not going within."

Bellamy holds the distinction of being the first actor who was able to leave the lot at a decent hour, and the first actor to have a stand-in at Columbia. Under tyrannical studio head Harry Cohn's reign, this was not an easy feat. How did he do it?

"Well, there were some four-letter words connected with that,"

Ralph Bellamy in an early eighties publicity shot.

answered Bellamy with a smile. "He spoke pretty gruffly and used a lot of profanity. I discovered that if you gave back as good as he gave ... he liked it, he smiled and you got your way. The first thing I got was a stand-in. I had to have a stand-in, we were working on so many different films at the same time. Stand-ins were something new in Hollywood. And I remember Harry saying over and over again, 'We've never had a stand-in

on the Columbia lot and we never will have.' I said, 'Well, tear up my contract because I can't work without a stand-in.' All this took quite a while
in his office. He finally said, 'All right, you have a stand-in under one condition. Don't tell Jack Holt.' That was easy because I'd never even met Jack
Holt. So I ended up with my stand-in.

"In those days we worked at all hours," continued Bellamy, remembering the primitive pre–union conditions in Hollywood. "There was no
Screen Actors Guild, no rules, and you could be called in at any time and
worked until any time, which we did. And I went up to see Harry again.
I knew him pretty well by this time. I got on with him. And I told him that
I would have to quit work at six o'clock. And he said, you . . . a little bit
of profanity . . . New York actors coming out here, we've never had that
on this lot and we never will have. So, again, I said, 'Then tear up the God-
damned contract!' After that I was able to quit at six o'clock unless it was
night work. Again, I had to promise not to tell Jack Holt that I could leave
at six o'clock," laughed Bellamy.

"We used to work on more than one movie at a time. It was very con-
fusing and slowed up all the shooting because you had to readjust in so
many ways. To begin with, you had to wear different clothes. And then
you had to take on the other character. And all of this took time.

"Working conditions, of course, were the main reason for starting up
the Screen Actors Guild. We had many meetings at people's houses, a few
of us, and it grew. The membership expanded, and finally we had enough
members to make a declaration—which we did. That declaration was,
'Either give us proper working conditions or we strike.' And they did."

Bellamy was one of the founders of the Screen Actors Guild and was
on its first board of directors. He was also the president of Actors Equity
for four terms (1952–1964). "FDR and I each had four terms," he noted
with a laugh. Some members of Actors Equity came backstage one night
and asked me if I would run for the presidency. And I said, 'I won't run,
but if you want to put my name up there, that's all right.' And I won. I
also won the next three terms."

Bellamy remembered one other time Harry Cohn became enraged.
It was during the shooting of *His Girl Friday* (1940), which also starred
Cary Grant and Rosalind Russell. There was one point in the script when
Cary Grant's character was asked to describe Bellamy's character. Grant
ad-libbed the now famous line, "He looks like that fellow in pictures — you
know — Ralph Bellamy."

"I believe Cary came up with that one," said Bellamy. "I wasn't working that next day, but I went over to the studio to say hello, and ran into
Harry Cohn on the back lot. Harry wanted me to go look at the previous
day's rushes with him. We went up to his private room, and Cary's ad-lib
came on screen. Harry screamed, 'What the hell are they doing on that

set? Where did that ad-lib come from?' He stormed down to the set and was madder than hell at them for interfering with the script. The line ended up staying in the movie anyway."

One of his best-known films, which also starred Cary Grant, was *The Awful Truth* (1937). Bellamy says the actors didn't even have a script to work from while shooting the classic screwball comedy. "Our director, Leo McCarey, would arrive each morning with notes written on some kind of brown wrapping paper. That was our script. He'd instruct, 'Okay, Ralph, you come over here, and I'll run the dog through here,' and so on. I tried like hell to get out of it the first day," Bellamy recalled about the role which would garner him an Academy Award nomination. "Cary even offered to do another picture for *no pay* if Harry would let him out of it. Irene Dunne cried, begged and pleaded to get out of it. We almost shot the whole picture that way. We learned our lines day by day, and shot the picture in just six weeks."

Bellamy almost always lost the girl to the leading man in films such as *Carefree* (1938), *The Awful Truth* and *His Girl Friday*. When I reminded Bellamy that he did get the girl in *Dance, Girl, Dance* (1940) with Maureen O'Hara, he said with a chuckle, "I've done 107 feature pictures, and so many of them I don't remember anything about."

One leading lady he did remember with a special fondness was Carole Lombard, his costar in *Hands Across the Table* (1935) and *Fools for Scandal* (1938). "She was just like heaven. Carole was just the way she appeared on screen. She was open and funny . . . and had a beautiful sense of humor. She worked with you. She listened to you . . . and I'm talking about acting. She listened to you when you were speaking. It was a delight to work with her. Just a delight."

During the mid-forties, Bellamy left Hollywood to go to New York, where he worked on the stage, giving performances on Broadway in *Tomorrow the World*, *State of the Union*, *Sunrise at Campobello* and *Detective Story*. At the time, he was also shooting his weekly television series *Man Against Crime*.

"Television in those days was interesting. It was a whole new field to begin with. We shot our show on kinescope, and of course, TV not having developed, there was no chain across the country. They mailed the kinescope to all the other towns that used it," reminisced Bellamy.

"We did *Man Against Crime* from Grand Central Station in New York. None of the studios had been prepared for television at the beginning. And they had been experimenting with TV upstairs at Grand Central Station. In addition to our series, they did *The Ford Theater* and *I Remember Mama* from Grand Central. There were just two studios, and they managed to bring off all three shows.

"*Man Against Crime* was the first private eye show, and we were

Bellamy as he appeared in the first weekly TV detective series, *Man Against Crime*, in 1950.

copied several times. And I know one thing . . . I had a short vacation and my wife and I went to England. I wanted to buy a trench coat. And I said to the salesman, 'I want everything that you can put on the coat . . . front, back, chest, shoulders—everything.' And he said" (Bellamy went into an English accent, imitating the salesman), "'You mean one loike Danny Kaye's?' And I said, 'Yes, I do.' I wore that trench coat as 'Mike Barnett.' And I think I was the first private eye in a trench coat. From that point on, most private eyes wore trench coats."

Much in the same way that James Bond would later introduce himself as "Bond, James Bond," Mike Barnett used to always say, "Mike Barnett, with two t's," whenever he introduced himself on *Man Against Crime*.

Believe it or not, in the days of early television, cigarettes used to be sent to hospitals as gifts for veterans. Bellamy remembers doing a live commercial for Camel cigarettes on *Man Against Crime*.

"The last thing I did on the television show each week was a blurb about next week's show. And then I said, 'Each week *Man Against Crime* is sponsored by Camel cigarettes. Each week the makers of Camels send gift cigarettes to hospitalized servicemen, servicewomen and veterans. This week's Camels go to....' And then I would frankly read a list of hospitals. And while I was doing this one night, gratuitously, I took out a package of Camels from my pocket and took out a cigarette, put it in my mouth and lit it, while I was talking. And when I got to the hospital part, I got a piece of tobacco stuck in my throat. Well, you can imagine — there's nothing you can do about this except cough it up, which I wouldn't dare do with a Camel cigarette on the air. I had to keep on talking. I couldn't say it was a Chesterfield or a Lucky Strike because everyone in the audience saw me light up a Camel. So I kept on talking," he laughed, "and by the time I finished reading the list of hospitals, tears were running down my face. I still have a kinescope of that commercial."

Bellamy was starring in *Detective Story* on Broadway during the same time he was doing *Man Against Crime*. After he shot the television show, he had to rush over to the theater to get there just in time for the curtain to go up for *Detective Story*.

"When I finished shooting *Man Against Crime* on Friday nights, they always had the elevator doors open wide, ready for me to rush through. I ran downstairs and got into a police car, which they would always have waiting for me. I pulled the siren, and we raced down the stage door of the Hudson Theater. We crashed into a fire engine one night. Nobody was hurt. And I just had time to run upstairs and change clothes into the character for *Detective Story*, and go downstairs and onto the stage. I was on stage for the rest of the evening. So, that was quite a day for me!"

Here's some good news for *Man Against Crime* fans: There is talk of possibly bringing the show back, according to Ralph Bellamy. "I believe they ran the show under another title for a while. I don't remember the title at the moment. It's being talked about for revival now — modernized. In its time, *Man Against Crime* was not a bad show. I don't know whether it will come off or not. I have nothing to do with it. But there is talk of bringing it back."

Among Bellamy's greatest artistic achievements is his role as Franklin Delano Roosevelt in *Sunrise at Campobello*, on Broadway in 1958 and on film in 1960. Although he knew FDR, Bellamy also did extensive research for the role. He found a man with the same affliction as FDR's at the

Institute for the Crippled and Disabled. He exercised with him every day before rehearsal.

"I had a wheelchair and crutches at home and used them in order to feel at ease, natural in the role," explained Bellamy. "I also knew FDR personally, and over a period of time, I had been invited to the White House for dinners and cocktails. So I had met and managed to be close to him. I watched his mannerisms—physical as well as speech. There was a danger of overdoing it, which I tried to avoid. But that was a terrific experience on the stage . . . a marvelous experience."

Bellamy won both the New York Drama Critics' Award and the Tony Award for his gripping performance in *Sunrise at Campobello*. He said that he believed he was the first person to give a long acceptance speech for an award.

"When I went up to get the Tony Award, I said, 'I want to publicly thank my wife for putting up with me through this long period of preparation and running all 'round the house in a wheelchair and crutches.' That started this business of everybody thanking everybody, like their families and friends," he chuckled.

In 1983, Bellamy reprised the role of FDR in the television mini-series *The Winds of War*. Some of his later roles, which are best known to film audiences, include a devil-worshipper in the guise of a kind neighbor who lives upstairs from Mia Farrow in *Rosemary's Baby* (1968), and the rather mean-spirited rich man who tries to take advantage of Eddie Murphy in *Trading Places* (1983). Don Ameche played Bellamy's brother in *Trading Places*. The two had great comedic chemistry together—even as unlikable characters.

Earlier in his career, an attempt to avoid an unlikable role resulted in his one professional regret.

"I turned down *Chinatown*, admitted Bellamy. "The script the director sent me was from page one—incest. And I'm no prig, I'm no prude, but it just did not seem worthwhile doing a role that would be denounced even if it were well done. I didn't want any part of it. John Huston finally played the part and received an Academy Award for it," he added with a laugh.

His most moving experience, professionally, was when he received his honorary Oscar in 1987, an award long overdue.

"It was a remarkable experience. When I walked out and that entire audience stood up, I choked up. I had to wait a second to pull myself together. To see an entire, enormous audience stand up for you is something that's just unexplainable. It was unexpected and very much appreciated."

And very much appreciated, respected and admired is exactly what Ralph Bellamy—who died on November 29, 1991—will always be to audiences everywhere.

Angela Cartwright

Series: *Make Room for Daddy*
Role: Linda Williams (1957–1964)
Series: *Lost in Space*
Role: Penny Robinson (1965–1968)
Series: *Make Room for Grandaddy*
Role Reprisal: Linda Williams (1970–1971)

With her dark hair pulled back in a pony tail tied with a ribbon, wearing frilly little dresses with ruffles and bows, adorable five-year-old Angela Cartwright as Linda Williams captured the hearts of millions on the Danny Thomas TV series *Make Room for Daddy*. She wasn't the wide-eyed Shirley Temple type, but sassy, with some of the best wisecracking lines in the script.

The kids on *Make Room for Daddy* (Angela Cartwright, Rusty Hamer and Sherry Jackson) were different from children on other sitcoms. They were streetwise, from New York, and knew their way around. The children had little arguments among themselves just like their fans did at home. One great "promo" the cable station Nickelodeon runs for the program shows Angela smashing a checkerboard over Rusty Hamer's head. How many little sisters do things like that every day? Realistic scenes like these were one reason so many people identified with the show.

Angela Cartwright was born in England, where she lived until she was just one year old. Her family then relocated to Canada. By the time she turned three, her parents had made the decision to build a life in the United States.

"We moved to Los Angeles, because my Mom and Dad both had a dream of coming to America. We came over on a boat. I mean it was like ... here we are immigrating to America," laughs Angela.

"My mother really wanted to live by the beach, so we moved to El Segundo in California. Our neighbor in the apartment building we lived in had children that were in show business. I remember that they did commercials. This neighbor told my Mom that she really should take my sister and I to see her agent. The agent really liked us, and signed both my sister Veronica and myself. We both started working right away."

11

Angela Cartwright

Following a small role in the Paul Newman film *Somebody Up There Likes Me* (1955), Angela landed the plum role of Linda Williams in *Make Room for Daddy*. The show had already been on the air since 1953 with Jean Hagen in the wife and mother role of Margaret Williams. When Hagen left the show, they killed off the character. Marjorie Lord was cast as Danny Thomas' girlfriend, nurse Kathy O'Hara. Angela portrayed her daughter Linda. Eventually Danny Thomas' character married Kathy, completing the family unit, which also consisted of daughter Terry, played by beautiful Sherry Jackson, and a son, Rusty, portrayed by the late Rusty Hamer.

It wasn't too long after she joined the show in 1957 that Angela began to receive record amounts of fan mail, particularly unusual for a small child. As Linda she was saucy, cute, and showed a lot of spirit for such a little girl, which is probably one reason she was so loved by children and adults alike. Angela was at one time receiving 200 fan letters a week and had 100 fan clubs.

"I remember that I signed a lot of pictures, knew there was fan mail and rode in parades, but I never had any awareness of the impact of what was going on," explains Angela. "It wasn't until I was much older that I became aware of what was happening.

"My parents treated me like a regular kid and that helps in how well adjusted you are. My childhood was never a nightmare like some child stars. I came from a really strong family unit. My parents were united together. People still recognize me. A lot of people grew up with that show

A wedding scene from *Make Room for Grandaddy* (1971). First row left to right: Rusty Hamer, an unidentified actress, Angela Cartwright, and Amanda Randolph. Second row: Danny Thomas and Marjorie Lord.

and are the same age I am, and they're still familiar with me today. It never ceases to amaze me how many lives television touches."

During the years that *Make Room for Daddy* was on the air, the audience watched Angela grow from a five-year-old child into a young girl of twelve. Reflecting on the success of the program, Angela says:

"*Make Room for Daddy* was a fun show to do. We filmed it in front of a live audience. There's nothing like playing off the response of a live audience. We had a lot of fun together. They were all like a second family to me. I can remember that it was really hard to say goodbye when the show ended. I can still remember the goodbye party . . . it was very painful because the cast had become such a big part of my life."

One of the cutest episodes of *Make Room for Daddy* which featured Angela was "Linda's Tonsils," in which Linda is afraid to get her tonsils out and Danny has to reassure her. The kid yells and screams and is stubborn as any real kid would be in that situation. Another funny episode, when Angela was a little older, was "A Promise Is a Promise," in which Linda goes on the *Art Linkletter Show* after Danny yells at her. Since the character Danny is an entertainer, and bad publicity could be damaging, he's afraid of what his little girl might say about him on the air.

My interview with Angela Cartwright was conducted before her fellow cast member and former child actor Rusty Hamer shot himself in despair. One thing Angela said rings true for many child actors, who, like Rusty Hamer, found that their early celebrity status was a hard act to follow as an adult.

"A lot of actors who worked in television as children left their series and then never worked again. All of a sudden they have to go back to school and fit into a regular schedule. Having to leave all that excitement cold turkey and go back to school is really difficult."

As is often the case with performers, Angela was basically a shy child. Having been tutored three hours a day on the set for most of her life, she found it difficult to go back to school. This was something she had to do by the time she reached her senior year in high school.

"Academically I fit in, but it was hard socially because all these kids had been friends for years," elaborates Angela. "I had this buddy, Maureen, who lived on the same block as me. I don't know how I would have made it through my childhood without her, she was great. We were best friends and did normal 'kid' things together. I did know some of the kids in high school ... some really wanted to be my friend and others wanted nothing to do with me. Maureen was wonderful and never treated me differently.

"Basically my life was in one sense as normal as it could have been for a working kid. I didn't hang around just with adults. I did have a childhood. I did have friends. The schedule on the Danny Thomas show was flexible. I didn't have to work every single day. On Mondays there were readings of the script; on Tuesdays we blocked it; on Wednesdays we blocked it with the cameras and on Thursdays we shot it. On Mondays and Fridays I was able to go to school."

After the *Make Room for Daddy* series ended in 1964, there was one problem that Angela, as a child actress, didn't have to face: staying active professionally. Almost immediately she was cast in the film classic *The Sound of Music* (1965) as one of the Von Trapp daughters. It's of this phase of her career that Angela seems to have the fondest memories.

"*The Sound of Music* was a great adventure for me. I made a really good friend on that film, Heather Menzies. She's married to Robert Urich now. I remember we were both Beatles crazy at the time. We stayed a month in Salzburg. There were six of us kids in the film—it was like a fraternity," recalls Angela.

"We were mischievous and had a lot of laughs together. We were just like kids in the school yard in the way that we got rid of our excess energy. We had to be disciplined during the day, but when you're a kid you still have that energy and fun-loving nature. At the hotel where we stayed we were terrors. I remember that people used to put out their shoes to be cleaned and we'd change them all around," she adds with a laugh. "We threw water balloons out of windows at people . . . things like that."

Following *The Sound of Music*, Angela was cast in the science fiction TV series *Lost in Space*. She portrayed Penny, the teenage daughter of the orbiting Robinson family. This role lasted for three years. After *Lost in Space* went off the air, Angela did various guest shots on other series, including playing Chip's girlfriend on *My Three Sons*. In 1970 she reprised her role of Linda Williams in *Make Room for Grandaddy*. The series sequel was short-lived, lasting only one year; however, Angela had not ever really been out of the public eye since the original show ended in 1964.

Since the 1970s, Angela has done some modeling, guest star roles and various nostalgia TV specials, including one she hosted with Jerry Mathers ("Beaver") of *Leave It to Beaver* and Jay North ("Dennis") of *Dennis the Menace*. She has also starred with other former child stars in TV movies like *Scouts Honor* (1980) and *High School U.S.A.* (1983).

Angela Cartwright has grown up. The little girl with the bobbing pony tail has matured into a raven-haired beauty with the same sweet smile and laughing eyes she had as a child. In 1976 Angela married musician-turned-businessman Steve Gullion and now has two children of her own—Rebecca, born in 1981, and Jesse, born in 1985.

Angela says her children have watched her in *Make Room for Daddy* and *Lost in Space* reruns. "My son Jesse is just starting to realize how strange it is to see Mommy as a little kid. It's hard to understand. None of us think of our parents as being kids!" laughs Angela. "It's interesting that our kids today are being raised on video. They're used to seeing themselves on TV. Whereas twenty-five or thirty years ago to see yourself on television was really amazing."

Would Angela allow her own children to become actors?

"Yes, I probably would. It would depend on the project. When I was a kid it was a lot different. Danny Thomas was really part of the beginning of television. To have a small child on a series was very unique at that time. It just wasn't done. Then there was a big spurt of it—Andy Griffith, Joey Bishop and Dick Van Dyke joined in and all their shows had little kids in their casts. Danny was kind of a ringleader in that whole thing."

Shortly after her marriage, Angela and her husband decided to go into a business venture together. They opened a beautifully decorated, unique gift shop called Rubber Boots in Toluca Lake, California.

"I remember that at the time I didn't want to sit by the phone and wait for acting jobs. I wanted to do something creative—an outlet—and this store has turned into something very good," says Angela with enthusiasm.

"I wanted this store to be like no other store I had ever seen. There never seemed to be the combination of being able to go to one place and buy not only for kids but adults as well, and games as well as serious gifts. I also wanted really good selection of cards that were from individual artists rather than a line of Hallmark or American Greetings. That's basically what I've kept over the years. It's kind of like a treasure chest of different things. I constantly change the merchandise. I carry Crabtree and Evelyn Soaps, foods, frames, hand-knitted sweaters, candles, a large selection of stationery and jewelry from all over the world. Shoppers can take care of more than one person in the store rather than go to a lot of different stores."

As far as her acting career goes today, Angela feels she'd be best suited to play a mother. "I'd like to do something worthwhile . . . a production with quality. It doesn't matter really whether it's comedy or drama. I did bow out for a little while to raise my children and run the business, but I'm still open to a good acting offer."

A lovely lady who enjoys her family and career, Angela Cartwright seems as though she'd be happy doing anything creative, whether it's running her "treasure chest" of a gift store or acting.

Opposite: The orbiting Robinson family from *Lost in Space.* Left to right: Angela Cartwright, Mark Goddard, Marta Kristen, the Robot, Jonathan Harris, June Lockhart, Guy Williams and Billy Mumy.

Barbara Eden

Series: *How to Marry a Millionaire*
Role: Loco Jones (1957-1959)
Series: *I Dream of Jeannie*
Role: Jeannie (1965-1970)

Barbara Eden will forever be known as the ravishing genie that every man fantasizes about. This beauty with her silky blonde hair and blue eyes (a real genie from Baghdad wouldn't exactly look like this), wearing her little pink harem outfit, exits and enters her bottle (decorated in 1960s mod decor) with pink billows of smoke. Barbara Eden and her beguiling genie character represent the best of sixties television fantasy.

It's interesting that on both *I Dream of Jeannie* and the similar hit series *Bewitched*, the male lead on the program would never allow his beautiful blonde witch or genie to utilize her unique powers. A man in real life would probably jump at the chance to have a gorgeous, magical woman make him the richest or most successful man in the world. But the characters of Tony Nelson and Darrin Stephens wouldn't hear of it, and were very adamant about their wishes — not that the woman in either case paid the slightest attention. But of course, without conflict there is no plot. A show about a person who gets everything he desires without any effort or any trouble resulting would get pretty dull after a while.

There is no question that both actresses who starred in these fantasy series were and still are beautiful. Elizabeth Montgomery has a cool, classy, Grace Kelly look. Barbara Eden is an exceptional beauty . . . exotic and sultry. These adjectives are usually reserved for sensuous brunettes. However breathtaking Barbara, with a fun-loving, sexy twinkle in her eyes, manages to combine the best of smoldering beauty with an innocent, effervescent "girl next door" quality.

One thing *I Dream of Jeannie* had that *Bewitched* did not was a mortal besides male lead who knew about the female lead's unearthly powers. On *Bewitched* there was no mortal but Darrin who knew Samantha was a witch. On *I Dream of Jeannie*, Bill Daily's character of Major Roger Healey not only knew Jeannie had magical powers, he was even human enough

Barbara Eden

to take advantage of them once in a while. Bill Daily did a marvelous job as the comically nervous, bumbling best friend of the leading man. Daily would later play the same sort of role (an absent-minded airplane navigator who didn't seem to know his right from his left) on *The Bob Newhart Show*. Daily is now a TV food and restaurant critic in Arizona.

Barbara Eden was born in Tucson, Arizona, and raised in San

Barbara Eden as every man's fantasy genie — the mischievous "Jeannie."

Francisco. She still retains fond memories of San Francisco, and recently married realtor Jon Eicholtz at the church where she was baptized in the city by the bay.

She says that her first show business aspiration was to become a singer, and she continues to sing today, when her schedule permits, at the best hotels of Lake Tahoe, Las Vegas and Atlantic City.

"For as long as I can remember, I wanted to sing — that was my first love. I studied at the conservatory in San Francisco," explains Barbara wistfully. "What actually led to my acting career was something my mother said to me once while I was singing one day. She said, 'Barbara, you're singing all the notes perfectly, but you don't mean a word of what you're singing. I think you should study acting.'

"So I auditioned for, and received a scholarship to, an acting school my mom had heard about on the radio. I began to get parts in plays. I remember thinking, 'Gosh, I like this a lot!' and, by the way, learning to act did improve my singing."

Following one year of working in San Francisco, Barbara moved to Los Angeles, and soon found work in a theater as well as a few small roles on television and in films. On the rerun circuit you can catch Barbara playing Elinor Donahue's alluring teenage friend on *Father Knows Best* in the episode "The Rivals." She even had a guest-starring role in *I Love Lucy*. In the episode "Country Club Dance," she played a sexy young thing who catches the eye of both Ricky and Fred, only to be set straight by Lucy and Ethel. You can also catch her on *The Andy Griffith Show*, in the episode "The Manicurist," as a curvy, loquacious manicurist who arrives in Mayberry by bus and proceeds unknowingly to captivate every man in the small town, much to their wives' dismay. Part of Eden's charm in almost all her roles, particularly the early ones, is that she doesn't seem to be aware of her beauty — there's no egotism at all — which makes her likable to women as well as men.

Barbara's first big break on television came when she landed a starring role on the series *How to Marry a Millionaire*. In this series Barbara reprised the Marilyn Monroe film role of "Loco Jones." As you may recall, "Loco" was a seemingly dimwitted, nearsighted blonde who would stumble into walls rather than wear her glasses. It was in *How to Marry a Millionaire* (which lasted two seasons) that Barbara first showed her comic promise. She would later bring some of the lovable, zany qualities of Loco to her role as Jeannie.

On *I Dream of Jeannie*, Barbara was magical and mischievous. She had the best of intentions, yet somehow hilarious mass confusion would break out in every episode. The popular program was often slapstick and frenzied but always very funny. *I Dream of Jeannie* has never been off the air since its inception in 1965. The show ranks right behind *I Love Lucy* in popularity and longevity with viewers. This in itself is an enduring testimonial to Barbara's talent as a comedienne.

While *I Dream of Jeannie* has been flying high in syndication, Barbara has starred in many television movies such as *Return of the Rebels* (1981), *The Stepford Children* (1987), *The Secret Life of Kathy McCormick* (1988), and *Your Mother Wears Combat Boots* (1991). In 1985, when Barbara starred in *I Dream of Jeannie: 15 Years Later* (with Wayne Rogers taking over Larry Hagman's role of Major Nelson), it was widely heralded that

Eden and Larry Hagman in a scene from *I Dream of Jeannie*.

Barbara had the same measurements as she did in 1965. "Before" and "after" pictures confirm that Eden's stunning figure hadn't changed a bit. There was one notable difference in the later version of the shows: Barbara was finally allowed to show her navel while wearing her revealing harem costume. NBC censors hadn't allowed her to show it twenty years before. "My poor belly button was discriminated against," says Barbara.

Jeannie, by folding her arms and blinking her eyes, accomplished some pretty amazing feats on *I Dream of Jeannie*. In the episode "Always on a Sunday," she turned every day into Sunday, just because she wanted to have her "master" home with her, and almost stopped the world from functioning since no one went to work.

She did some creative baking in a couple of very funny episodes. In "My Master, the Swinging Bachelor," she baked a cake that made everyone who ate it act like a child. All the actors in the episode seemed to have fun with that one. In "Jeannie and the Wild Pipchicks," Jeannie's mother's homemade candies, "Pipchicks," cause everyone's hidden desires to come out. Not something to be served at your next dinner party, unless you want things to get very interesting. Incidentally, in this episode and a couple of others, Eden played her own mother, with hysterical results—a kind of "yenta" genie.

One might wonder, looking at Eden today, if she has the fountain of youth somewhere in her backyard. One might also guess, considering those acclaimed measurements, that Barbara never eats more than a meager carrot stick, but actually she adores Mexican and Chinese food and has a great passion for a rich dessert. "I eat out often because I am not a very good cook. And I'm crazy about chocolate souffles . . . I love them! I love them! I love them!" says Barbara with a laugh.

Those who were disappointed that Barbara was not re-teamed with Larry Hagman in *I Dream of Jeannie: 15 Years Later* did get to see the two actors reunited on Hagman's mega-hit series *Dallas* in 1991. In a delicious plot line, Eden's character, Lee Ann De La Vega, gets to turn the tables on her former "master" by taking over nasty J.R.'s company, and then proceeds to hire him as *her* employee. When one of the characters asks, "Why did you hire him?" Eden answers matter-of-factly, "To keep a close eye on him, and it will be easier for me to make his life totally miserable."

Barbara portrayed Jeannie yet again in the 1991 TV movie *I'm Still Dreaming of Jeannie*. With Larry Hagman's astronaut character presumably in orbit, Ken Kercheval (J.R.'s nemesis from *Dallas*) played Jeannie's "temporary master" leaving the door open for a new series.

Eden has also starred in two other television series—*Harper Valley* and most recently *Brand New Life* with Don Murray. In the series *Harper Valley* Barbara reprised her role from the feature film *Harper Valley PTA* (1978), which grossed close to 30 million dollars. Barbara has come full circle from reprising Marilyn Monroe roles to reprising her *own* roles.

Barbara Eden is both vivacious and enthusiastic. She takes great delight in talking about a wide variety of topics and punctuates many of her sentences with an appealing giggle. Barbara doesn't have a "star" attitude; she's genuine and quite appreciative of any compliments that come her way. Taking time out from rehearsing a Bob Hope special, Eden discussed her career, and in particular her *I Dream of Jeannie* success.

"I had no idea *I Dream of Jeannie* would be on the air for this long. Actors seldom think about how long what they're doing is going to be around. I'm always surprised when I see myself on TV," she says. "Sometimes I'll see myself on screen, and I'm rather taken aback. It's like looking in the mirror. I'm not one who likes to watch myself on the screen. But I can watch *I Dream of Jeannie* now. Enough time has passed that it's almost like watching someone else. Actually, my favorite role was in the film *The Seven Faces of Dr. Lao* (1964). I loved it because I got to play a frustrated, plain school teacher," adds Barbara, laughing.

During the original run of *I Dream of Jeannie,* women's lib activists were up in arms over the series, particularly over Jeannie calling her boyfriend "Master." When asked about that now, Barbara laughs: "She really was the one in control, wasn't she? It's true that Jeannie was always saying 'Yes, Master,' but then she'd go and do exactly whatever she pleased anyway. It didn't really matter what *he* had to say about it. She was really very liberated in that sense! Jeannie really was the strong one on that show. *She* had the courage and the imagination."

Since she performs live in addition to her film and television work, Barbara explains how the two compare: "There is a difference, of course, between performing live and doing film. You just switch gears, and use different techniques. A performer needs to know how to do both, or it's like using just one leg. You need to use both legs to have a healthy craft."

Looking back on Barbara's roles so far, the majority have been "good," albeit mischievous, characters. There is the exception of her portrayal of Jeannie's comically evil sister on *I Dream of Jeannie.* As the evil Jeannie, Barbara wore a black wig (just as Elizabeth Montgomery wore a black wig as her naughty look-alike cousin, Serena). It seems the old western rule of good guys wearing white hats and desperados wearing black hats held true in the sixties for both actresses. The good girls were the innocent, golden-haired heroines, and the bad girls were raven-haired minxes. This plot device did give Eden and Montgomery a chance to showcase different sides of their comedic abilities. As far as portraying villainesses or heroines, Eden has this to say:

"I think it's important to play in a project that is well-written. It doesn't really matter whether the character is good or bad. I guess I never really have played a villainess. It might be fun to play evil roles because they get more interesting and shocking things to do. I would play a villainess if the part was well written. I've come to greatly value the written word and the director, believe me. I've always wanted to do something of George Bernard Shaw's. I don't know if the networks would think it was very saleable or commercial, but his plays certainly are entertaining and wonderfully written."

Barbara finds time to work with several charities despite her heavy schedule, including the American Cancer Society, the March of Dimes, the American Heart Association, and the Wellness Community, a place of great inspiration and hope, where the late Gilda Radner and others who are ill have found strength to deal with their diagnoses, through the support of other patients who are in the same situation.

"The Wellness Community in Santa Monica (California) is a holistic place for people who are considered terminally ill by the medical profession. People go there to socialize, and to have visualization and group therapy. They go to plays, movies and bowling. There's a positive thinking philosophy there to try and make people well and improve the quality of life. It's wonderful, and they've had many people who have recovered. We all know we're going to die, we just don't know when. As long as we're living, let's improve the quality of life we have — that's what the Wellness Community is all about," asserts Barbara quietly.

Quality is extremely important to Barbara in both her personal commitments and her professional choices. So, whether Barbara Eden is playing the genie, the boss or a character in between, you can be sure she will always be entertaining. There is no question that Barbara Eden is a woman and performer of rare quality.

Kathy Garver

Series: *Family Affair*
Role: Cissy Davis (1966–1971)

The 1960s series *Family Affair* was a favorite of children and adults alike, a pleasant interlude from the confusion and turbulence of the times. Each week the sentimental program began with a colorful kaleidoscope and festive music, followed by episodes written with sincerity, warmth and humor.

Family Affair centered around an independent bachelor, Bill Davis, played by whiskey-voiced Brian Keith, who adopts his recently orphaned nieces and nephew. The adorable six-year-old twins, Buffy and Jody, were played by Anissa Jones and Johnnie Whitaker. Stately British actor Sebastian Cabot played Mr. French, the very proper butler, who ended up a reluctant but lovable "nanny" to the children. Imposing and strict on the outside, with a soft-hearted undertone, Cabot's Giles French was one of TV's finest substitute mothers. Those kids wouldn't dare misbehave when he bellowed (in a sophisticated British sort of way, of course), "Children!" Kathy Garver portrayed the model teenager, the perceptive, sweet-tempered niece Cissy Davis, with a professionalism beyond her years.

Kathy shone in both the comedic and dramatic scenes on the show. Since she was older than the other children and more mature as a performer, Kathy was able to add the dimensions of sadness and tenderness to her role as an orphan. Her soft brown eyes mirrored the pain any 15-year-old would have felt in such a desolate situation. This is particularly evident in the first couple of episodes of the show. In "The Gift Horse" and "Jody and Cissy," Garver's character Cissy feels that her uncle only wants to have the younger children live with him. She played her scenes as Cissy with great sensitivity and very effectively, a teenage orphan with a stiff-upper-lip facade covering for a young girl who feels abandoned and doesn't wish to be separated from her younger brother and sister.

Family Affair is still popular and is currently being aired in syndication on cable television. Today, Kathy Garver is as lovely as ever. In one pretty, petite package is a producer, writer, voice-over artist and actress.

Kathy Garver

On a cloudy, gray Saturday morning after brewing a cup of tea for her husband (who she suspected was coming down with a cold), a bright and energetic Kathy talked about her beginnings in the entertainment industry:

"I started acting professionally at the age of seven. I began taking singing and dancing lessons when I was two years old from Ethel Meglin of the Meglin Kiddies, so I've been doing this a long time," she explains with a slight chuckle.

Cecil B. DeMille was the first to sense the potential of Garver's talent.

A scene from *Family Affair*. Left to right: Kathy Garver, Johnnie Whitaker, unidentified actor, Brian Keith and Anissa Jones.

He originally hired her for a small role in *The Ten Commandments* (1956). However, he was so taken with her that he had special scenes written into the film specifically to showcase little Kathy's budding talent.

"I was featured in *The Ten Commandments* and had a semi-regular role on a show called *This Is Alice*, but actually *Family Affair* was the steadiest and most prestigious thing I did as a child or teenager.

"The set on *Family Affair* was really fun to work on. Not only were the actors wonderful to work with but the crew members were great too. They were always playing pranks on us. I remember one time I was in a scene where I was supposed to reach under the bed to get Brian Keith's slippers. So, I reached under the bed and pulled the slippers and they wouldn't move. Well, it turned out that the crew had nailed the slippers to the floor," laughs Kathy, who went on to remember her series co-stars Sebastian Cabot and Brian Keith.

"Sebastian Cabot was the consummate professional, and was very dedicated to what he was doing. He worked very hard. It was difficult for

Garver as the model sixties teenager, Cissy Davis.

him to memorize, so he would spend the weekend poring over his lines and getting them *just so*. This was in great contrast to Brian, who would just look at a page, instantly memorize it, and go off and do his thing. He changed words here and there, but he got the gist of what the script was conveying. Sebastian and Brian were very different in style, but very compatible in the way that it finally came out on screen."

Having recently watched *Family Affair* again Garver reflects, "Seeing the show again after so many years . . . I realize what a gentle show it was. And they really endeavored to have long, long close-ups, and the pace was very slow, so much more than anything you'd find today. It's more methodical than even I was aware of, at the time. *Family Affair* was a fantasy, an idealized type of thing. But the slow pace of the show afforded viewers an opportunity to get to know the characters well. You were able to empathize with them—and as I say, it was very gentle. It was very different in that aspect than any other show that was produced then and now. It had that very special quality to it."

Garver, who has two brothers and one sister, was the only member of her family to decide on acting as a career. Since she started in show business dancing and singing when most children are working on walking and talking, one might wonder if she ever found herself feeling as though she missed out on a normal childhood. Kathy recalls:

"No, I didn't miss out on anything because my parents were very adamant about the fact that I would have a normal childhood. When I would work they would tell me, 'Don't tell anyone at school where you are or what you're doing.' So, it was really kind of kept quiet. Actually, it took me a long time to admit, 'Yes, I am an actress.' It was so ingrained in me not to brag or make an issue about being on television. I was able to pursue all the normal teenage activities like being a cheerleader in high school and college. And I enjoyed all the social clubs and sororities."

After *Family Affair* went off the air in 1971, Kathy starred in an Israeli musical stage version of the series, followed by one year of study at the Royal Academy of Dramatic Arts in London. Kathy returned to the United States to portray Eliza Doolittle in *My Fair Lady*, and she has gone on to act in sixty television shows, forty commericals and eight feature films. Approximately nine years ago, she became interested in the production end of the business. Kathy received rave reviews for her work as the star and producer of *Vanities*.

"I co-produced *Vanities* with James Doolittle at the Doolittle Theater. We toured both the East and West coast with the play. My character, Joanne, aged from 18 to 24 to 28. I really loved playing that role, exploring the different stages of the character's development. It was a very rewarding experience.

"I, personally, find comedy easier than drama. And even though a lot of actors say that comedy is more difficult, for me there's an easier release doing comedy, even though it has a serious undertone. That's what makes it funny—you have to take it seriously when you play it. Comedy is also easier for me to do with body movements. With drama when you take the same emotion it becomes histrionic—I think—if you use the same kind of physical movements. In comedy it just becomes funny."

In recent years, with a degree in speech, and of course a wealth of acting experience behind her, Kathy is beginning to do some work in audio cassette and voice-overs. She played Mother Goose on a *Mother Goose Rhymes* audio cassette. Kathy's version of "Mother Goose" is now available at the Metropolitan Museum of Art. She will also be producing and narrating the *Tales of Beatrix Potter* series for audio cassettes. One of her voice-over parts on film was that of the demon in *The Heretic*, quite a switch from Mother Goose and Cissy, and obviously a change that takes a talented actress who can portray a great range of characterizations.

As an actress, Kathy has completed a guest star spot on Andy Griffith's *Matlock* series and a role in *Crimes of Passion II*. "ABC couldn't get advertisers for *Crimes of Passion II*, evidently they thought it was too violent. So I bounce back and forth between bunnies and violence," she laughs.

"I've never done villainess roles, because I don't look like a villainess. I really do enjoy doing evil, evil parts in voice-over. It's just that I'd never be cast that way. Even if I had the greatest make-up man in the world, I'd still have a baby face, which doesn't make for a believable villain.

"I also do a lot of voice work on cartoons and write lyrics for children's songs. I have developed a couple of other projects because you have to have your fingers in many pies in this business. We have a pilot that we're doing in tandem with TMS, an animation house. It's a half-hour sitcom that I wrote with a partner," she explains. "It's interesting — whenever I start to write, whether it be songs or scripts, I always write in dialogue. I think it's ingrained in me because I've been in the business so long. I really enjoy putting things together. I like to see the big picture as well as the details. I've never had the desire to direct, but I like to write and love to produce."

Garver has also hosted several talk shows and a radio travel show. "I did enjoy that experience, and I'm glad that I did it for a while. There's a lot of research to be done when you do a talk show. Of course, the guests weren't always predictable. It was exciting doing the real 'live' type of interview on a show. I enjoy doing voice-overs and acting now more than doing the talk show hosting."

As many of us do when we leave a job, Kathy lost touch with her colleagues once the *Family Affair* series ended. "Since I live in San Francisco, when I come down to L.A. I'm so busy with my business and my family that I don't get a chance to see various people I've worked with. The only ones left from the *Family Affair* cast now are Brian and Johnnie," she says quietly, with sadness in her voice.

Sebastian Cabot died in 1977. And during the summer of 1976, Anissa Jones (Buffy) died tragically at the age of 18 from a drug overdose. Brian Keith has since starred in various television series, including most recently *Hardcastle and McCormick*, and a recurring role on Burt Reynolds' *Evening*

Shade series. Johnnie Whitaker (Jody) is active with the Mormon Church in Utah. Several years ago, Whitaker spoke about Anissa Jones. He mused on the differences in their real-life childhood experiences — she grew up in a broken home, while he came from a strong, supportive family — and acknowledged that he was dismayed, but not very surprised, about her death.

In 1990, Whitaker made an appearance on *Geraldo*, Geraldo Rivera's talk show, where he spoke further about the death of Anissa Jones. He said that Jones was left for dead at 2 a.m. by her so-called friends — people who were also involved in the drug culture in Oceanside, a Southern California coastal town. Apparently, Jones didn't actually die until approximately 5 a.m. There was a hospital right around the corner from where she was when she took the overdose. If the people she was with had called an ambulance or taken her to the hospital, Anissa Jones might be alive today.

Kathy Garver is still recognized as Cissy today. "People always say that I look familiar to them. And my husband usually tells them it's because I was on *Family Affair*, and they say 'No, that's not it.' It's cute because they argue about it. Usually I end up having to tell them that I never did go to their hometown high school," laughs Kathy.

"*Family Affair* was a nice, quality show, and I like the fact that they used film," says Kathy, with the producer part of her creative personality kicking in. "They don't do very many sitcoms on film these days; it's primarily all done on video tape. I think film always gives a different kind of reality to a program. I like that aspect of the show. It was a quality production, and very well done."

Kathy Garver resides in the Bay area with her husband, David Travis, and her infant son, Reid Garver Travis, who was born in February 1991.

In addition to her busy professional schedule, she still finds time to serve on the advisory board of the Humane Society, work with the Family Services Agency in San Francisco and play in celebrity golf and tennis tournaments to benefit various charities.

How does she manage her professional activities, taking care of an infant son and her charitable endeavors?

"You have to be very organized," she says with a smile. "You have to make lists every night and get things ready, laid out, for whatever you're going to do the next day."

A creative dynamo, Kathy would someday like to act in another sitcom, do dramatic mini-series roles and continue with her voice-over work, writing and producing.

Gale Gordon

Series: *Our Miss Brooks*
Role: Osgood Conklin (1952–1956)
Series: *The Brothers*
Role: Harvey Box (1956–1957)
Series: *Sally*
Role: Bascomb Bleacher (1958)
Series: *Pete and Gladys*
Role: Uncle Paul (1960–1962)
Series: *Dennis the Menace*
Role: John Wilson (1962–1963)
Series: *The Lucy Show*
Role: Theodore J. Mooney (1963–1968)
Series: *Here's Lucy*
Role: Harrison Otis Carter (1968–1974)

A distinguished veteran of countless radio and television shows, Gale Gordon has one of the most familiar faces and voices in show business. Mention his name and people invariably smile. Gordon, who often plays the ultimate overbearing authority figure, is usually cast as someone's comically cranky boss, principal or landlord.

Gordon is a master character actor, and a genius at the art of comic timing. We all remember him bellowing at stars in the shows he's been featured on. However, he can also get a laugh without uttering one word. His facial expression conveying complete exasperation says it all.

There was one great scene in the "Lucy's Substitute Secretary" episode of *The Lucy Show* that refers to Mr. Mooney's explosive temper. The scene has Lucy telling a temporary secretary (Ruta Lee) about her banker boss, Mr. Mooney:

Lee: What kind of boss is your employer, Mr. Mooney?
Lucy: Let's put it this way, he's more boss than employer. He yells a lot.

Gale Gordon

Gale Gordon was born into the theatrical profession. Both of his parents were actors. His father was Charles T. Aldrich, and his mother was Gloria Gordon.

"My father was a vaudevillian, and my mother was principal boy in pantomime among other things such as light musical comedy. She was also in television years ago with Marie Wilson in *My Friend Irma*. My mother played the landlady, Mrs. O'Reilly. . . ." Many will also remember Gloria Gordon from Jack Benny's radio program, where she played one of his fan club members who happened to have a crush on him.

Although the child of actors, Gordon's first ambition was not to be an actor but a dancer.

"Actually, I wanted to be a toe dancer," he laughs. "My mother did an act in London. She had two girls who did a little ballet number while she changed gowns between the songs she was performing. And when the ballet slippers wore out, she brought them home to me. I put them on and could walk all over the house on my toes, up and down stairs and everything else. The toe dancer phase lasted only for a short time, as long as my mother was doing the act with the ballet dancers."

Gordon, a grand comedian, would later utilize his dancer's dexterity in some hilarious physical comedy bits with Lucille Ball. Who could forget the sight of stuffy, impeccably dressed Mr. Mooney turning cartwheels, dancing the cha-cha or falling through a trap door?

"The last thing in the world I should have done was go into the theater because I was inordinately shy as a young man. I couldn't open my mouth. At a party, I was the one stuck up against the wall. I was embarrassed about talking. I felt that I couldn't talk well," explains the modest actor, whose resonant speaking voice and flawless diction are now instantly recognizable to audiences.the world over.

Amazingly, there was a time when doctors thought Gale Gordon might not be able to speak at all.

"My voice, I have to say, is kind of miraculous because I was born with a cleft palate," he confides. "As a matter of fact, my first trip to England was when I was eighteen months old. My mother knew of a doctor in London who specialized in repairing cleft palates to a great extent with children. It was a very, very serious thing in those days. So my mother, being English, took me back to England for the operation to repair the split roof of my mouth, which almost developed into a harelip but was prevented by this operation. The fact that I can talk at all is a miracle. I don't have anything in the back of my throat, there's no uvula. The doctors look at it and they get dizzy. It's a bottomless hole. It's only by the grace of God that I can talk at all."

Remembering his early days in theater, Gordon continues, "I started out at the bottom, by the way. I didn't have a speaking part and made just fifteen dollars per week in a play off–Broadway. And then as I got into it, and began to learn lines and get parts, I found that when I knew what I had to say, I had absolute confidence. Everybody I knew as a young man used to say, 'This man has no nerves!' Well, I was as nervous as anyone else, but I had the confidence of knowing what I was going to say. That confidence helped me through a great many trials and tribulations, and finally made the nervousness worthwhile."

Through the twenties and thirties, Gordon continued acting on stage, both in Los Angeles and in New York. He performed on Broadway with Maria Ouspenskaya in *The Daughters of Atreus* in 1936. A film, *Death Valley Days* (1937), followed his Broadway performance. Gordon proposed to a lovely actress, Virginia Curley, who appeared with him in that film. The couple married in 1937, and they still act together on stage every year at the Stage West Dinner Theaters in Canada.

Many long-running radio roles followed his film and Broadway work, including Mayor La Trivia on *Fibber McGee and Molly*, the sponsor on *The Phil Harris and Alice Faye Show*, and the banker, Mr. Atterbury, on Lucille Ball's *My Favorite Husband*. He also had the title role in *Flash Gordon*.

One of his radio roles which would later become a popular television character was Osgood Conklin, affectionately known as "Old Marblehead," the blustery high school principal on *Our Miss Brooks*. That series starred Eve Arden.

"Eve Arden was a dear, dear woman. That part came on radio in 1946. I remember that it was 1946 because it was a year after I had gotten out of the service," says Gordon. "My wife, while I was gone, had decided that since I had missed out on so much during the years I was in the service, I ought to establish a fee, a salary, and not do any show for less than that certain fee. As it happened, I had left in the middle of doing *Fibber McGee and Molly*, and had come back to that show. They paid me $150 a show, and that was a lot of money in those days. I was grateful that my job was waiting for me when I came back from the service. So I went to work for them and got my $150 a week. And then other people would call and offer me $50 or $25 a show, which as a salary was very small even in those days. I turned them down. When I'd tell people that I wanted $150 they almost fainted," he chuckles. "They thought I was an upstart and an egomaniacal idiot. Months went by, and I was terribly depressed. Finally, a man called from CBS. He said, 'We're doing a summer replacement show with Eve Arden, and there's a part we'd like you to do.' I said, 'That's very nice.' And they said, 'How much do you want?' I replied, '$150 a show.' He shouted, '$150 a show!' and almost fainted. I'm sure he had a mild stroke. He said, 'CBS cannot pay that amount of money.' So that was that.

"My wife and I went on a brief vacation at Santa Ysidro Ranch near Santa Barbara, California. While we were there, we heard the first radio show of *Our Miss Brooks*. We both looked at each other when the show was over, and Virginia said, 'Thank God they didn't pay you the $150 because that's the worst show I've ever heard.' They had a high school principal on there who was barking like a dog, and speaking in improper

Gale Gordon and Eve Arden in a scene from *Our Miss Brooks*.

English, which is one thing that just drives me crazy. We were just congratulating ourselves when the producer called the next day and said, 'All right, we'll pay you the $150. We want you to do the part.' They hadn't liked the man who played the role. And that was how I got the role on *Our Miss Brooks*. The only episode I didn't do was the first one."

Gordon's wife, Virginia, played the original Mrs. Conklin on *Our Miss Brooks*.

"She played the role on radio and for the first year of the television series," says Gordon. "But we were in an automobile accident, we were rammed by a truck while we were on vacation. She had a whiplash and had to give up the role. She never went back to it. However, she was the original Mrs. Conklin."

Quite often, both adult viewers and teenagers actually confused Gale Gordon with the principal he played on *Our Miss Brooks*, as well as his other bossy characters.

"Very often people would stop me on the street and ask, 'Why are you so mean to Miss Brooks?' The audience took it very literally. People still do that today. They expect you to be funny on a moment's notice or, in my case, get angry. Once I had a woman stop me and say, '*Please*, yell at my children!'" Gordon laughs heartily at the memory. "People forget that it's all put on. We're pretending! In those days, many people thought that all the comic dialogue was said on the spur of the moment. They couldn't believe that people rehearsed this, that writers actually wrote those lines for someone else to say. They thought we just made it all up as we went along."

Gordon remembers the set and people involved with *Our Miss Brooks* with great warmth.

"The whole troupe was like a family. Gloria McMillan, the girl who played my daughter Harriet ... her father died when she was quite young. When she got married, I stood up for her, and gave her away," he remembers with obvious tenderness. "Also, Eve had a Christmas party every year just for the cast. To avoid buying presents for everyone, we'd draw names out of a hat, and buy a gift for the person in the cast whose name we had drawn. This made shopping very exciting—trying to figure out what to get for Dick Crenna or Janie Morgan. The holidays were very important to Eve. She'd bring a Christmas tree down to the studio during Christmas week. We'd have treats and goodies.

"I went to her services, of course," he added quietly. "It was for me like losing a very close and dear friend, which, of course, she was. I feel very fortunate to have worked with such delightful people like Eve and Lucy. Great talent and great ladies. It's extremely rare to find talent and friends like they were."

Gordon is filled with admiration for many of the actors he's worked with over the years.

"I've had high regard for a great many actors. I started out as a serious actor. I didn't start out as a comic actor at all," admits Gordon. "That just developed because I happened to be louder than anyone else. If they wanted a blowhard character, they called on me. I've had innumerable people that I've respected and venerated. As a matter of fact, in later life, I got to play with some of them, which delighted me.

"I remember on *Here's Lucy* we did an episode with Richard Burton. Lucy and I were both thrilled to work with someone of his caliber. He was utterly charming and delightful, and so was Liz Taylor. I had admired Richard Burton for years and years before I had ever worked with him. He was a great, great actor. It was a joy to get to know him as a person.

"I also worked in several scenes with Basil Rathbone in the Sherlock Holmes radio series he did with Nigel Bruce. And that was wonderful, because here were two English Gentlemen . . . and Basil Rathbone had this great ability as an actor. But they were both like two school kids at play when it came to the radio show. They were getting paid, they thought, to do something that was terribly, terribly amusing — reading off of a piece of paper instead of memorizing lines. But they were both like two naughty boys. It was a complete revelation for me to see Basil Rathbone, who was the epitome of dignity, class and charm, acting like a kid! They (Rathbone and Bruce) were unequally delightful!"

Certainly one of the people Gordon admired most was his dear friend Lucille Ball. He worked with her on *The Lucy Show* and *Here's Lucy* for a total of eleven years. Gordon's distinguished bearing and Lucille Ball's wild antics meshed perfectly. They were an unbeatable team. Among the things that impressed Gordon the most about Lucille Ball were her perfectionism and her ability to work harder than anyone else.

"Lucille would never allow anyone to double for her. If she had to learn how to ice skate, she'd ice skate. If she had to go down a staircase on skis then that's what she'd do," elaborates Gordon with admiration. "She wouldn't allow a double to do it because the cameras were very close. She thought it would be ridiculous to use a double. None of us *ever* had doubles do stunts for us. If I fell in the mud or got stuck in a hunk of cement or fell down a trap door then that's what I did.

"Lucille didn't care about messing herself up. A lot of stars of her stature wouldn't do physical comedy because they were afraid they'd get their hair messed up or they'd look bad. I remember once she fell into a vat of green dye. She came out with not only her hair green but *everything* was green! It was tremendously funny to see her come out all green, but it took hours to get her cleaned up and her make-up put on to do the rest of the show. But things like that were important because they looked real. And this is very, very important when you're doing comedy. You've got to believe that it is happening and it has to be real.

"The secret of comedy, if I may be so bold as to make a statement like this, is that for comedy to be good it has to be played straight. And again, the greatest example of this is Lucy Ball. No matter how wild the shows were that we did, no matter how bizarre the situations were, they were never played as if they were funny," continues Gordon. "They were played like serious incidents of ordinary everyday life. And that's why they are

Gordon and Lucille Ball in front of the Christmas tree in a scene from *The Lucy Show*.

terribly funny and are still considered classic comedies. What's wrong with most of the comedies nowadays is that the actors know they're funny or think they are. That takes away from the comedy right away. The ones who play comedy straight are the great ones—the ones people love to watch."

As much as he is identified with television, Gordon prefers the stage to film and television work.

Alan Hale, Jr., teaching Gordon a dance in an episode of *Here's Lucy*.

"I think anybody who has been in the theater, prefers it. Television is a . . . factory. You turn out things on a revolving assembly line. You don't have time to perfect anything in television. If you're doing a weekly series it's very difficult to make each episode of the series as good as it should be because you don't have the time to devote to it. This was one reason that Lucy was such a hard worker, and many people didn't like going on her show because they worked from the moment they got there until the show was filmed. And that was four days," Gordon explains. "And in those four days we had to learn the show and do all the camera rehearsing, because there were three cameras in each scene all going at once.

"Guest actors had to rehearse with us as performers because each word that an actor might have said might be a cue for the camera to move or turn in order to get a different angle. All those technical things that television requires take away from the concentration that you should be giving the character itself. For that reason, Lucy worked very hard for the four days. The results show. Her work has endured for some forty years or more because she was never satisfied. She would never say, 'Oh, we can get by with this, it won't matter,' because if it mattered to one viewer— that would have ruined it as far as Lucy was concerned. And that's why television is a sausage factory. Radio wasn't so bad because you didn't have to memorize the lines. But you did have to do everything because your own character was in your voice—that took a little doing. Most people thought that if you could speak English or read then you could be a radio actor. Well, that wasn't so. You had to put a great deal into your reading to convince somebody who was just listening that a certain character is speaking."

One memorable role Gordon had in between *Our Miss Brooks* and *The Lucy Show* was as the irritable neighbor of Dennis on *Dennis the Menace*. Joseph Kearns had played George Wilson on the show previously, and passed away during production. The producers decided to bring in a new character, the brother of George, whom they called John Wilson.

"I enjoyed working with Jay North. I've always enjoyed working with people. I've worked with very few that I considered unpleasant. *Dennis the Meance* was a joy to work on," reminisces Gordon. "Jay, at the time, was eleven, playing a nine-year-old. He was terribly embarrassed about having to wear that little jumper suit. He fretted a little about that. Jay and I got along beautifully. We had fun together. It was great fun, and there was a friendly family feeling with that troupe too. And that's terribly important when you see a cast of people who are together for a long time or even a short time. If there's friction among the cast members, I think it shows in the final result."

Although he has a home in the Hollywood area, Gale Gordon has spent most of his time in the Southern California community of Borrego Springs.

"We've lived here about forty-six years now. We have one hundred acres here," says Gordon about his "Tub Canyon Farm." "I don't have to hear anyone's television or radio. It's what I've always wanted. My wife and I love to read. We're going to have to move out to make room for the books! And we have our dogs ... we're very happy here."

Gordon continues to make television guest appearances and is still passionate about his work.

"I've never been bored in my life working," he asserts. "A lot of people get bored after five minutes. They want to go home and pick up their check. That's never been the case for me. I'm always the first to arrive and the last to leave because I truly enjoy what I'm doing. That's why I've been in show business for so long—I love it!"

When real-life bosses and neighbors are cranky, one wishes they were also as funny as Gordon's characters. Gale Gordon is a warm, familiar friend whom audiences everywhere have enjoyed having in their living rooms for decades. Future generations will continue to delight in his performances through the magic of syndicated television.

Don Grady

Series: *My Three Sons*
Role: Robbie Douglas (1960–1972)

For a dozen years during the sixties and early seventies, the family television series, *My Three Sons* warmed the hearts of its worldwide audience, not only with laughter, but with a special kind of camaraderie between brothers as well as father and sons. And even though the programs have messages (as all good sitcoms do), they never come at the expense of entertainment. Now airing on cable television several times a day, *My Three Sons* continues to entertain viewers twenty years after going off the air. The late Fred MacMurray, with his cardigan sweater, bow tie and pipe, still has all the right answers for a whole new generation of kids.

The original cast of the series featured MacMurray as widower Steve Douglas (possibly the most patient, calm father in the universe); William Frawley (fresh from *I Love Lucy*) as Bub, the boys' grandfather; Tim Considine as Mike, the oldest son; Stanley Livingston as the youngest son, Chip (affectionately called "Chipper" by his father); and Don Grady as the middle son, Robbie.

The boys were portrayed realistically as rough-housing brothers who sometimes fought but still loved each other. As teenagers they were always shown on the telephone, a classic portrayal that will probably never change no matter what the day or age. Considine, Livingston and Grady literally grew up before viewers' eyes as boys, teenagers, and finally as married men during the dozen years *My Three Sons* was on the air.

Grady's character of Robbie usually did all the things he was supposed to do. Like the other two sons, he was a good kid. In the episode "The Wrong Robbie," Grady got to play a dual role as Robbie and his cocky, sports-car-driving double, who gets him in all kinds of trouble. The double kisses girls all across the campus, and is nasty to just about everybody he sees. Of course, no one believes this boy isn't Robbie until the end of the episode. Grady seems to relish the role of the double. One other notable episode of Grady's is "My Son, the Bullfighter," in which Robbie, insanely jealous of a bullfighter on whom his girlfriend has a crush, takes up bullfighting himself. Grady's hilarious scenes with the bull are among

47

Don Grady

some of his best work in comedy. (This episode co-starred handsome Latin actor Alejandro Rey, who later starred with Sally Field in *The Flying Nun* as the playboy who is constantly irritated by Fields' flying nun character. Rey died in 1987 at the age of 57.)

Grady's Robbie married Katie, played by beautiful blonde actress Tina Cole, who brought a great deal of charm and warmth to the role. The TV couple then had triplets, which would have established three sons for the series for the next twenty years, if it were to go on. This would actually give a producer endless possibilities for a reunion movie today.

Grady left the series towards the end of its run. To accommodate the actor's absense, the character of Robbie was sent to South America on business while Katie remained home with the triplets. One promo the cable station Nickelodeon ran for *My Three Sons* exclaimed, "Katie has triplets, Robbie moves to Peru!" In real life, moving to Peru might be a tempting proposition if you had three babies screaming all at once.

William Frawley left the series in 1964 because of health reasons (he died in 1966) and was replaced by William Demarest, who portrayed Bub's sailor brother, Charley O'Casey. Both Demarest and Frawley played cantankerous mother figures in the all male household. Demarest's Uncle Charley was far more cross and bossy than Frawley's Bub, who was also shown to be crusty, but was somehow a more sentimental character.

After Tim Considine left the show in 1965, Barry Livingston (Stanley's younger brother) joined the cast as Ernie Douglas, which re-established the three sons needed for the show's premise. Barry had a recurring role as a neighbor boy, Ernie Thompson, before Considine left the show. The Douglas family adopted Ernie at the beginning of the 1966 season. The new season brought other notable changes for *My Three Sons*. The show switched networks from NBC to CBS, and went from black and white to color.

Before his role on *My Three Sons*, Grady was a Mouseketeer who co-starred on *The Mickey Mouse Club* under his real name, Don Agrati. Don's first love is music, and he was something of a child prodigy. It was his acccomplishment in music that ended up impressing the people at Disney, and this marked the beginning of his long career.

"I started composing and writing songs when I was 14 or 15 years old," reflected Don on a cloudy but cozy Monday morning. "I was a musician first . . . that's how I got started. I practically started playing the drums when I was coming out of the womb," he laughs. "Our home was filled with music. My parents played the accordion, and they gave me a set of drums when I was two and a half years old. By the time I was eight or nine, I could play eight different musical instruments.

"My career really started when I went on an audition in San Francisco for the Mouseketeers. They were looking for a couple of new Mouseketeers in 1957. For the audition I played a bunch of these musical instruments. They liked that because they could use me playing any one of these instruments for different spots on the show." Grady also played trumpet, drums and guitar on various episodes of *My Three Sons*, and wrote several songs that were used on the show.

And it's the music industry rather than the acting profession that Grady has chosen today as his career. "It's funny because I started out with the Mouseketeers, and now I'm doing the songs for *The New Mickey Mouse Club*," says Don. "My wife Ginny is another great thing Disney

A 1969 cast shot from *My Three Sons*. Back row, left to right: Fred MacMurray, Beverly Garland, Don Grady, Tina Cole, Stanley Livingston, and Barry Livingston. Front row: Tramp, Dawn Lyn and William Demarest.

brought to my life. I met her while working on a show for Disney five years ago."

Don and his wife, Ginny, have a toddler son, Joey, who was born in 1990. They live in the San Fernando Valley area of Los Angeles. Grady is obviously a proud father who loves to talk about his young son. He says that becoming a father is the most exciting thing that's ever happened to him.

Grady's musical work consists primarily of film scoring. He is a keyboardist and has his own synthesizer studio. "When I do film scoring I do a lot of different styles and types of music depending on the mood of the piece," explains Don. "I enjoy jazz and rhythm and blues, and I love to write ballads."

Recently, Grady scored *Switch* (1991) and *Skin Deep* (1989), both Black Edwards' films, and an action TV show called *The Edge and Beyond* with James Coburn. He says he's done everything from Playboy awards to children's songs. In addition to scoring, Grady also worked on all three of Sam Riney's jazz-fusion albums. Don's most recent album is *Victim of Emotion* on CBS Portrait. You'll also find one of Don Grady's songs on the soundtrack of *Girls Just Want to Have Fun.*

"I did the new *Donahue* theme. Phil Donahue's theme song is my composition" says Don with enthusiasm. "I did a documentary in 1991, with Tom Selleck and Whitney Houston hosting, called *Over the Influence,* about kids coming off of drugs. It was incredible because I had 53 minutes of music to write and orchestrate in two and a half weeks. I discovered during that time that I could sleep for four hours a night and not get too sick," he adds with a slight chuckle. "I've also done a lot of work for the Universal theme parks. I did "The Riot Act," which is music for the western stunt show up there. It's a forty-piece orchestra type of thing, which we pre-recorded, and they play it at every show. And we did the music for the "American Tale" attraction, which is based on the movie of the same name.

"After I did *My Three Sons,* I recorded an album called *Homegrown* for Electra in 1975. And then I started to miss acting again, so I went on the road and did the national tour of *Pippin.* After about a year of stage work in New York, I realized that I missed songwriting and music so much that I had to make a decision that I was going to do one or the other . . . either continue acting or work on my music. I made the decision to do music. It was a tough choice, but music is something I really love. The music comes easy to me."

Don Grady's appearance has changed very little over the years that *My Three Sons* has been off the air. A handsome man, Don has the same friendly smile, cleft chin and vivid blue eyes that won over all those teenage girls in the sixties. He is still recognized as Robbie today.

"It's interesting. I'm recognized more out of town. In L.A. everybody is pretty cool about it. When I'm out of town I get a lot of recognition, especially now that *My Three Sons* is on Nickelodeon. It's amazing that a whole new group of kids is watching the show now. Hopefully, I won't get so old that no one will recognize who I am," Don laughs.

Did Don enjoy the recognition when he was a teenager?

"I went through three phases. I really enjoyed it at first because it was a real rush. Then I went through my second phase when I didn't like it because I felt like I didn't have any privacy. After the show was off the air for a long time (before it came back on reruns) I was wondering why no one recognized me. Then I went through my third phase, wishing people knew who I was again."

When asked if fans or the people who recognize him have any misconceptions about his life, Don says:

"Most people seem to think that I live in an 'Actor's Heaven.' They think I'm above the normal everyday things we all go through. I'm not. I've got to wake up in the morning and go to work just like everybody else. But most people don't look at actors that way, I guess. People think that once you have some fame you're a little bit different than everyone else, but that's not the case."

Don has stayed in touch with his *My Three Sons* co-stars. He says he sees Stanley and Barry Livingston all the time. He called Fred MacMurray every Father's Day, right up to that actor's death in 1991. After a long period of not seeing his show, Don has started watching reruns of *My Three Sons* again.

"I started videotaping the shows so I'd have them for my grand-children or whatever," he says with a chuckle. "Once in a while I'll take a look at them. They're pretty good. It surprises me how well they've held up considering they were made so long ago. We did so many episodes over a twelve-year period that sometimes I'll watch one, and I won't even remember doing it. I'll say to myself, 'I don't remember saying that line,' or, 'Who is that actor?'

"We did the show very strangely, because we did it all around Fred MacMurray. We did all his scenes and close-ups first. He only worked three months out of the year. Then we'd go back and pick up all of the other shots that we hadn't done in the episodes. Everything was done out of sequence. Sometimes we did twelve to fourteen different episodes in a day. You really had to stay on top of it."

There's one particular anecdote that Don shared about an episode he couldn't possibly forget. This show had to do with a lion escaping from the circus and making his home in the Douglas family's household.

"In this episode, Chip tells us all in the middle of the night that there's a lion in the house. Of course, we don't believe him. Anyway, while this lion was on the set, it got loose and the trainer told us all to freeze and not to move. The lion just walked around and we watched it. It was a real test of nerves. It finally got bored, and wandered away from us to the other side of the set. William Frawley, who had no idea what was going on, was whistling happily (as he always did) on his way back to the set.

"We (the rest of the cast) were still frozen in our spots. Poor Bill came face to face with this lion, and there was this long silence. And then suddenly he screamed, 'Oh, Shit!' Well, he ran really fast back to his dressing room, which was the worst possible thing he could have done. Fortunately, the lion didn't pounce on him."

Don Grady has many good memories, and is obviously a man very much at peace with the work he did as a child actor. He doesn't seem to have any particular axe to grind about the experience, but would he let his own son become a part of the acting profession? Don answers this question with refreshing candor and insight.

"That's a touchy question. It would all depend on how he feels someday. I really wanted to act, no one pushed me. It was my own desire that motivated me to do it," Don elaborates. "I have seen a lot of kids who are in the profession and don't care about it. They're really not interested in acting at all. Their parents think it would be great, the kids are cute and they are pushed into it. And God forbid that if these kids, who don't have any particular talent and don't want to be there in the first place, are successful. Because if they do taste that success . . . it's like a drug. And it's a tough one, especially for kids, to grow out of. And I think that's where a lot of the bitterness and resentment comes from. The general public doesn't want to hear this stuff. If you talk to a kid who was bitter, the public doesn't want to know about that. It ruins their conception of who that kid was, and it hurts their memories of what they were.

"There's no psychotherapist on the set. There's also no concern on the employer's part of what all this attention might be doing to a kid's mind. There should be some safeguards on that.

"There's no way that you can have a normal childhood when you're on a series. There's nothing normal about it because you are working every day. Different kids get different things out of the experience. Some child actors have very bitter memories, and are resentful about the whole thing. I think what they feel resentful about is not the experience, but the after-shock of not being successful, being finished with the series, and going on with their life not having all of that attention.

"For me it was a great experience. It gave me discipline and taught me to work in a professional manner . . . have my lines memorized. I really loved *My Three Sons* and missed it when it was over. But I was really fortunate because I had my music to turn to. Even though it was rough going for a while with music, it was something I could devote my time to and become involved with. Now everything's working out great, and I love what I'm doing. I feel pretty lucky about the whole experience."

Linda Kaye Henning

Series: *Petticoat Junction*
Role: Betty Jo Bradley Elliott (1963–1970)

Linda Kaye Henning is perhaps best known for her spirited portrayal of Betty Jo Bradley, the youngest of the three beautiful sisters on the popular CBS series *Petticoat Junction*. For seven years, Henning, a gorgeous, red-haired actress with a radiant smile, starred on the homespun situation comedy which took place in the mythical farm community of Hooterville.

Hooterville was also the setting for the *Petticoat Junction* spin-off *Green Acres* and had ties with *The Beverly Hillbillies*. Actors from all three programs made cross-over appearances on each other's shows. These entertaining rural comedies were among the most highly rated series of the sixties and early seventies.

The mother of the three lovely daughters—who had managed to give birth to a blonde (Billie Jo), a brunette (Bobbie Jo) and a redhead (Betty Jo) was Kate Bradley, owner of the Shady Rest Hotel, played with just the right combination of motherly love and humorous exasperation by Bea Benaderet. Uncle Joe Carson, the self-appointed manager of the hotel who was constantly involved in get-rich-quick schemes, was portrayed by throaty-voiced character actor Edgar Buchanan, a veteran of countless westerns and a real-life dentist who later decided on acting as a career. Buchanan as Uncle Joe, dressed in his checkered shirt, bow tie and dark sweater, was usually shown taking a nap on the front porch swing of the Shady Rest Hotel. Uncle Joe must have needed his rest, as he was most likely storing up his energy to go out and cause trouble (however good his intentions might have been) for the other characters. All three of his nieces were named after him—hence the "Jo" part of their names.

Linda's father, Paul Henning (once the head writer for *Burns and Allen*), was the executive producer of *Petticoat Junction* and all the other Hooterville-related comedies. Yet he was not the one who encouraged Linda to audition for the part of Betty Jo. Linda was working with Bea Benaderet's son, Jack Bannon, in a show put on by a young people's

Linda Kaye Henning

theater group. Benaderet was impressed enough with Linda's talent to suggest her for the role to Paul Henning.

"Bea pointed out to my father how much I was like the character of Betty Jo, and asked him to let me audition for it," recalls Linda. "Well, Daddy didn't really want me to do it because he didn't want people to say it was nepotism—that he was giving me the part because I was his daughter. So, he pretty much left it up to everyone else—Bea, the director at the time, and the producers. Bea had a lot of say regarding who was to play her daughters. I remember, I screen tested all day long. Daddy stayed out of it totally.

"In those days I didn't use my last name. My father didn't want me to. I used my middle name, Kay. He said I should just put an "e" at the end of it, and everyone would think I was Danny Kaye's daughter because of my red hair," continues Linda with a laugh. As a matter of fact, people would call out to me, 'Miss Kaye?' and I wouldn't even turn around. I never got used to it, and I didn't like it. Eventually, I put Henning back in my name. In a sense I understood my father's worry. He thought it would hurt me. People just assumed . . . the first year on the show people were, I think, kind of tiptoeing around me. They knew I was, in a sense, the boss's daughter. Actually my father didn't even write *Petticoat Junction*. He wrote the pilot and maybe one other episode. He was too busy doing *The Beverly Hillbillies* every week. He didn't have time to do *Petticoat Junction*. In those days, we did thirty-nine shows a year. There's only time to do so much.

"People learned that I was low man on the totem pole anyway. And you'd laugh if you knew what we were paid in those days compared to what actors are paid today. I was scared, eager, and working my way up. I made sure I was as professional as anybody could be. I'd arrive on time, knowing my lines, and I wouldn't give anybody any problems. That's how I learned. I spent seven years going to school . . . learning and working with some of the best character actors in the business."

Before *Petticoat Junction*, Linda had already acted in a couple of other pilots, including one based on the "Archie" comic strip. She also did guest appearances on *Mr. Ed* and *The Many Loves of Dobie Gillis*. While she was still in high school, Henning appeared as one of the teenage dancers in the film *Bye Bye Birdie* (1963).

Linda grew up in a world where she was literally surrounded by the glamour of show business. Much of her time, as a child, was spent in the company of television stars, but she didn't realize that they were famous— they were just neighbors and friends. A couple of these friends were George Burns and Gracie Allen.

"Yes, I knew them, but they weren't celebrities to me. They were just people that my folks knew. We learned to swim in George Burns' pool. I also knew Bob Cummings. My first little boyfriend, when I was about five years old, was Dana Andrews' son. I was over there all the time, but I didn't know Dana Andrews was a star. At the age of five it doesn't mean much anyway," she laughs. "I didn't know what being a big movie star meant— they were just nice people. And my father is the most unassuming man in the world. He could win Academy Awards—in fact he was nominated

A 1963 cast shot from *Petticoat Junction*. Pat Woodell, Jeannine Riley and Linda Kaye Henning.

for one — and nobody would ever know it. He doesn't toot his own horn. He has never been show-bizzy. He's very down-to-earth and very shy."

Linda originally began acting because of her own shyness. "At first, I wanted to be a dancer," explains Henning. "I studied ballet but I was painfully shy. My mother found out about a children's theater group, the Peter Pan Players, which she thought would be good for me. I was so shy I wouldn't look at people, I wouldn't talk to people. My first part was as the fairy godmother who turns into a cat in a cute version of *Cinderella*. The man who was in charge of the theater was really quite talented and wrote some of the plays himself. My brother, Tony, joined our group for a while. So did our neighbor, my brother's friend, a little boy named John Ritter. I've often said later that it's too bad we didn't have videotape in those days because I could have blackmailed the two of them . . . John and my brother running around in tights," laughs Linda.

In real life, as a child, Linda was very much like her tomboy character, Betty Jo.

"Even though I was an actress and ballet dancer, I used to run around a lot like a tomboy. I have a picture of my sister Carol and me standing with my brother. My sister and I look like the scroungiest, mangiest two kids you've ever seen, and here's my brother dressed like Little Lord Fauntleroy. I spent much of my youth in trees. I used to climb trees all the time and read. A couple of times I remember hopping down from my tree and almost scaring people to death who were walking up our driveway," says Linda with a laugh. "One time I left my brother in a tree. I climbed down and just left him there. My father was not thrilled because he and his writing partner had to go up and get him down. I've also always been crazy about animals. My father put that into the character of Elly May on *The Beverly Hillbillies* as well as into my character. Remember, the dog always followed me home."

For those *Petticoat Junction* viewers who might be racking their brains trying to remember the name of the dog on the show (who later became "Benji" of movie fame)—his name was "Dog."

Henning's character of Betty Jo often got the most interesting things to do on the show because she was a tomboy. While the other two girls might be worrying about dates, Betty Jo was likely to be learning how to drive the Cannonball (Hooterville's resident 1890s steam engine), tinkering with all things mechanical or out playing baseball. Linda played the role with great enthusiasm and freedom in a way that was reminiscent of Carole Lombard in the screwball comedies of the thirties. It didn't matter if Lombard was drenched or struggling with a fishing pole, she was still beautiful and endearing. Henning has that same quality.

Because of the tomboy aspects of Betty Jo, a couple of very funny shows were written showing her personality changes. In the episode "Betty Jo Goes to New York," she goes to the Big Apple with Eva Gabor's *Green Acres* character of Lisa Douglas (who always seemed to be dressed in a negligee). Betty Jo comes back completely transformed into a junior Eva. Henning was adorable in that episode. And in "Is This My Daughter?" she returns from Europe a changed woman.

Many sitcom characters have had babies on their shows—a big ratings booster—but not even Lucille Ball got to go into labor and drive a train (!) at the same time, as Betty Jo did in "The Valley Has a Baby." Henning actually has a real-life fondness for trains and loves mystery films that feature trains. "There's something very mysterious, exciting and romantic about trains. How fascinating it must have been when people used to travel everywhere on the train," she says.

One funny story Linda remembers from her *Petticoat Junction* days, concerns her looking very pregnant because of the padding she had to wear as Betty Jo.

"Every summer, while we were on hiatus, I would do musical theater. I had just finished doing *The Sound of Music* with a wonderful Austrian actor named John Van Dreelan. I didn't know it, but he knew Bea Benaderet. He came to the set and visited one day. It hadn't been that long

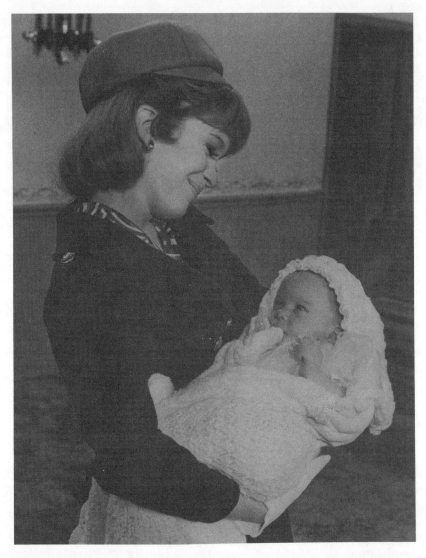

Linda Kaye Henning with her TV baby, Kathy Jo, in an episode of *Petticoat Junction.*

since we had worked together . . . maybe a few months at the most. He walked on the set and here I am looking nine months pregnant. I remember his eyes were really wide when he looked at me. I don't think he watched the show or knew that my character was pregnant. At that time, I was engaged to Mike Minor. We were married on the show but not in real life," explains Linda, referring to the actor who played pilot Steve

Elliott on *Petticoat Junction*. (The two married on the show as well as in real life, and then later divorced.) "Bea said to John, 'Here's Linda and her fiancé, Michael—they'll be married in a couple of months.' I remember John didn't say a word. I played his little innocent daughter in *The Sound of Music* and here I am looking very pregnant, introducing my fiancé. In those days that was not a common thing. It suddenly dawned on me why he wasn't saying anything," Linda laughs. "Then I said, 'No, no—this comes off!' while I removed all of my padding. That was so funny! In fact, everyone wanted me to go out to lunch with them when I wore my padding—because I'd keep the stomach on, wouldn't say anything, and we'd always get a table right away!"

One of the experiences she values the most from *Petticoat Junction* was the chance to work with Bea Benaderet. Benaderet, a master character actress, had done countless roles before *Petticoat Junction*, including various radio and television characterizations from *The Adventures of Ozzie and Harriet* (on radio) to the *Burns and Allen* and *Beverly Hillbillies* television shows. She was also the voice of Betty Rubble on the animated classic *The Flintstones*.

"Working with Bea was a wonderful experience," reflects Linda. "She was like a second mother to me. She was my teacher, and had faith in me. Bea was so helpful and I learned a lot from her. She would give me little hints of things along the way, and just by watching her I learned so much.

"It was very difficult when she was dying. She'd come back for a while and then she'd leave. We lost Smiley Burnette that same year. He played the engineer, and I worked a lot with Smiley because I worked so much on the train.

"One of my keenest memories of the show was the year that Betty Jo had the baby. Bea was too ill. She just couldn't do it. They recorded her voice to do different things. In the show, she was supposedly away taking care of a relative. My character was pregnant and sitting on the porch swing, and I get a letter from her. They played her voice as I'm reading the letter. It was so hard for me to do some of the shows, because I was so moved by what was happening to her. And the scene where I finally had the baby and Bea comes in . . . you just see the back of her head because it was a double. She was too ill to do the show. It was a very emotional time for all of us. Not only was it such a terrible shock losing the star of the show you're on, but she was my friend . . . a real example for me of a teacher, mother and friend. We were all determined that we were going to keep going for her sake, and we did."

Since *Petticoat Junction*, in addition to a couple of producing projects with her friend and former series co-star Meredith MacRae, Linda has acted in several television movies and in many guest-starring roles on series like *Hunter, Mork and Mindy* and *Happy Days* (in which she played a sexy nurse who examines "The Fonz").

Henning also had a recurring role on the series *The New Gidget*, playing an obnoxious mother of a teenage daughter. "I played the woman you love to hate. She was really awful and nasty but fun too. She and her daughter dressed alike—I mean down to the jewelry. As the show progressed, the writers really liked us. It was fun to come in and be nasty and mess everyone up. We always got ours too. We were such a tacky family," laughs the actress, who obviously prefers the more colorful villainess roles. "We would have worked more if the show had stayed on ... I'm sure. I would love to do a soap opera and play the rich bitch who screws up everyone's lives."

In addition to television, she's done quite a few musicals and theater productions such as *Bus Stop, Gypsy, Damn Yankees, Seven Year Itch* and *Applause.* Her greatest artistic triumph was playing Billie Dawn in *Born Yesterday* in New York. The role is very much identified with Judy Holliday, who won an Academy Award for it, and for that reason, it's not a role for an actress to take lightly. Linda wanted to bring something different to the part and not just mimic Holliday. She succeeded, with very good reviews, and credits director Cash Baxter with helping her find herself as an actress.

"I really think he was responsible for my learning to have faith in myself as an actress," says Linda. "He let me explore for several days into rehearsal, and let me find my own way in the role. I took a part not knowing what to do with it, and made it one of the best things I've ever done. I learned every single night I did that show, and I did it for eight weeks. It was a challenge and turning point in my life and my feelings about myself as an actress."

Henning also belongs to a radio theater group called California Artists Radio Theater, also known as CART. "We do plays on the radio. We have a theater now and they want us to do shows live, just like they used to do back in the thirties and forties. It's so much fun with the sound man doing all the sound effects, different people getting up to do different voices. We've done works by George Bernard Shaw, Oscar Wilde and Shakespeare. We've also acted in plays by Irish playwrights because a lot of members of our group are Irish and from the Abbey Theatre (Henning is also part Irish). Radio is different. Radio doesn't care what age you are and what you look like. Radio cares more about what you sound like and, most importantly, about your talent. I get to do a lot of things in radio that I wouldn't ordinarily have the chance to do," says Linda with obvious enthusiasm.

Henning's parents, Paul and Ruth, actually met on radio. Both were radio actors in Kansas City, Missouri.

"Daddy would write his own show, mainly because there was nobody else to write it. He would sing and do parodies of songs. My parents even acted on a soap opera together. That's how they met. The station manager said there would be no inter-departmental dating. So, of course they had to date," laughs Linda. "So, in a sense, that station manager was responsible for getting my parents together. They went to Chicago for a while before they got married. Then Daddy came out to California to work, and fell in love with it. He asked my mother to marry him and move to California. They got married in Yuma, Arizona. My mother had always wanted to be married under a palm tree. So they got married (they thought) under a palm tree, but it was really a cactus. They didn't know the difference!"

When not working as an actress or producer, Henning keeps busy with classes at UCLA, sign language lessons, and a great interest in archaeology. Because of her lifelong love for animals, Linda is also a volunteer at the L.A. Zoo. She gives tours, and she lectures and educates about the zoo, conservation and preserving species. "I love animals so much. I feel a real kinship with them. This is a way for me to give back to them. All during the time we did *Petticoat Junction*, Frank Inn, our animal trainer, would bring animals to me that were getting used to people on the sets. I'd always get to hold them and pet them. I wish I'd known about the zoo program ten years ago, I love it!"

With her many diversified interests, Linda Kaye Henning is certain to continue excelling in all her pursuits, whether educational or artistic.

Anne Jeffreys

Series: *Topper*
Role: Marian Kirby (1953–1955)
Series: *Love That Jill*
Role: Jill Johnson (1958)

A decade before witches, genies and martians were standard TV fare, Anne Jeffreys, "The Ghostess with the Mostess," and her husband, Robert Sterling, "that most sporting spirit," starred in the very first fantasy television series, *Topper. Topper* was based on the novel by Thorne Smith about a married pair of happy-go-lucky ghosts who must do a good deed in order to get into heaven. George and Marian Kirby had been too busy partying and living it up during life to have done anything which might be considered truly worthwhile. So as ghosts, they take it upon themselves to teach stuffy, staid banker Cosmo Topper (portrayed by Leo G. Carroll) what they know best — how to get some fun out of life . . . or death, as the case may be. Unlike other fantasy sitcoms in which only one partner had magical abilities, the Kirbys were evenly matched in the supernatural powers department. They were fun-loving, naughty and childlike, with only Topper around to try to keep them in check. Sterling, a superb light comedian, and the effervescent Jeffreys glided across television as lightly as any sprites, playing their roles to perfection.

One of stage, screen and television's greatest classic beauties, Anne Jeffreys started training for her impressive and varied career in the entertainment industry at the age of five. Jeffreys was an opera singer before she even thought of becoming an actress, and she feels a deep gratitude towards her mother — the independent Kate MacDonald Jeffreys — for the rewarding career she's enjoyed and excelled at all of these years.

"My father died when I was very young. My mother was the one who had the ambition. My talent was inherited from her. I come from a very fine old southern family, and they didn't approve of young ladies going on the stage," recalls Anne, who was born in Goldsboro, North Carolina.

"Since Mother was the first born and had a mind of her own," she adds with a laugh, "she would run off to New York and study theater.

65

When her money would run out, Grandfather would send her money to come home. But he would never subsidize her studies there. She became very discouraged. After several trips to New York, she happened to meet my father up there. He persuaded her to give up the idea of a career, marry him, and raise children. I was the third one born. Daddy and Mother were divorced when I was six months old. I never really saw him or knew him.

"My mother sacrificed strongly for my career. She was a brilliant person. She could paint, she could seam, she could act ... she could do anything. Mother took out her lack of being able to fulfill her own career and channeled that energy into me. Thank goodness she did. I was a very obedient child. I adored my mother and did anything she told me to do. I did not have the security or belief in myself. I just didn't have the drive for a career. She did all of that for me. And, of course, today I am very grateful to her. Sometimes when I was little, I would resent it because I'd say—to myself, never aloud—'I want to go out and play. I don't want to study my piano or go to my voice lesson.'

"So that's how I got into opera. When I was thirteen, Mother took me to New York. I worked there with a group called the Manhattan Opera Company. I studied voice privately with a teacher from Juilliard. When I was sixteen, I fell in love with my music teacher," continues Anne with a laugh. "So Mother decided it was time to leave, and she took me to California. That's how I got started in films."

As a little girl, Anne went to the movies often with her grandmother, who adored Nelson Eddy.

"Grandmother took me to all of the Nelson Eddy and Jeanette MacDonald films. She was in love with Nelson and I completely concurred with her opinion. I just thought he was the cat's meow.

"I remember once visiting my sister, who was then living in Hendersonville, North Carolina. They had an apple orchard there with many beautiful apple trees which were all in bloom. It was beautiful there. I remember I heard on the radio that Nelson Eddy had married. I was so disappointed and upset. I was about twelve ... maybe younger. I went out and climbed up into an apple tree and cried all afternoon. I cried because he didn't wait for me to grow up," says Anne with a laugh at the memory of her childhood crush.

Jeffrey's first big film was I Married an Angel (1942), which, much to her delight, just happened to star Nelson Eddy and Jeanette MacDonald.

"That was the thrill of a lifetime, believe me. Because I'd just come to Hollywood and I was very shy. I was taught that you didn't speak until you were spoken to ... and I had a very thick southern accent," reminisces Anne. "Nelson was very different than he appeared on the screen. He was very funny, and he even tap danced! He was very bright

Anne Jeffreys

and very warm. And, of course, when he came around me on the set, I was like the girl in *Annie Get Your Gun*, I couldn't talk. I was paralyzed. I remember on the last week of the film, I was sitting in the makeup chair one morning. Nelson had a photographer with him and walked over to me. He said, 'I want to take a picture with the quiet one.' Normally, I can't imagine being called 'the quiet one,'" laughs Anne, "but whenever he came around me—I couldn't talk! At the end of the picture, he gave me the photograph inscribed, 'To Anne Jeffreys, From Her Adoring Slave, Nelson Eddy.' And, let me tell you, that picture was carried around with me for years and years.

"I met him again, years later. He was doing nightclubs. I was in New York on Broadway. I came to see his performance, went backstage, and we had a very nice, long conversation. I asked him, 'Did you realize how smitten I was with you? I'm surprised I could even sing with you around.' I guess it's like the person who stutters. You stutter when you talk, but you don't stutter when you sing," laughs Anne.

Although she remembers the experience of working with Nelson Eddy as being a happy one, the actress remembers seeing herself on screen for the first time with less enthusiasm.

"It was terrifying," she says. "I die a thousand deaths when I see myself. To this day, I hate seeing myself on screen. The only reason I ever watch anything that I do is to critique my performances. I much prefer the stage to the screen. On stage you're your own master. There's nobody there to re-light or to edit. Your performance is what you're doing at the moment. It's much more gratifying. I've done fifty-four films and hundreds of television shows—but the stage is my first love."

Jeffreys also played Tess Trueheart in the Dick Tracy films of the forties. She remembers the films as being fun to do, but says she didn't take them too seriously at the time.

This vivacious actress counts three long-running musicals she starred in among the roles which have given her the most artistic satisfaction.

"I've enjoyed doing *The King and I* over the years. And I loved *Camelot*. I've done at least 600 performances of each of those. They're two of my favorite roles. Of course, I did *Kiss Me Kate* on Broadway for two solid years—887 consecutive performances.

"That was before I met Robert. I met him during my final days with *Kiss Me Kate* at the Shubert Theater in New York," remembers Anne about her handsome husband and frequent co-star, Robert Sterling. "Mother encouraged me to go out with Robert. I thought 'This is all I need—a good-looking, flip actor.' But Mother was in love with him. She said, 'This is the man you should marry and have children by.'" Her tone is wry, but Anne obviously adores her husband of forty years.

The couple have not only co-starred in two weekly television series but also have done nightclub acts, television guest appearances and film work together. Many marriages would crumble under the strain of being together all the time, but not the Sterlings' union.

"I remember when we first got the idea to do a nightclub act we knew a wonderful couple, Peter Lyn Hayes and Mary Healy. They had an interview show which they did from the Stork Club in New York. Peter Lyn and Mary said, 'Uh oh—you're going to do an act together?' We answered, 'Yes.' We were newly married, within the year. They said, 'Well, kids, forget about it, the honeymoon is over. When you start working together, the fur flies and that's it!' I said to myself, 'Oh, no.' I became hesitant about it. I didn't want my marriage to go on the rocks just because we were going to work together. It worked out completely the opposite way for us. We were very happy about working together. We get along very well, anyway. But we have never had any professional problems, ever.

"With the *Topper* series, it worked the same way. We used to laugh and say, 'We don't care who gets the close-ups—as long as one of the two of us does.' That was our attitude. We always joked about it, and enjoyed working together very much."

Jeffreys and Sterling had been married about two years and were in the process of touring the country with a highly successful nightclub act when they were first approached about doing the *Topper* series.

"I got a call from my agent saying, 'I'm going to send you a script. Would you two be interested in doing a television series based on the *Topper* movies?' I had been a big fan of the *Topper* film starring Constance Bennett and Cary Grant when I was young. I told my agent we'd love to do it. I thought it would be absolutely smashing and asked him to send a script," recalls Anne. "We got the script and just loved it. We came to Los Angeles to play the Coconut Grove, and while we were there we shot the pilot. We worked on the pilot during the day, and did our performances at the Coconut Grove at night. After we finished the pilot, we went on to San Francisco to play the Fairmount. They (the producers) called and told us to cancel the rest of the tour. They said that *Topper* was one of the quickest-selling series that had ever come about."

Jeffreys remembers the series as being a lot of fun, but very complicated technically.

"We had all the best special effects in the business for those days. And it meant prolonging hours of shooting because when you're working with all the special effects, it takes more time," explains Anne. "*Topper* has a big following still. People just love it who remember it. There isn't a day that goes by that I don't either get a letter from someone saying they were a big fan of the *Topper* series, or I see somebody someplace who says 'Oh, I loved that series!'"

Leo G. Carroll, who starred as Cosmo Topper, had done countless films of the thirties and forties before landing the title role in the popular television series. The British actor with the thick eyebrows, long face and faultless command of the English language once played a ghost himself— Jacob Marley, in the classic 1938 version of Charles Dickens' *A Christmas Carol*, which is shown on television year after year during the holidays.

"Leo G. Carroll was a love," says Anne. "He was very, very English, and very quiet and subdued and had sort of a dry chuckle most of the time. He looked rather dour, you know. He told us later that when he first came on the series, his wife was very, very ill. He hadn't confided in anyone, and I thought he was rather sullen before I knew about the situation. He didn't really speak or fraternize between scenes. He'd go sit in his chair and nod off, while they were changing the lights. And then he'd get up and do the scene. When we realized after a month or two what was troubling him, we became very, very close. We loved Leo dearly."

Jeffreys' favorite episode of *Topper* is one called "The Proposal."

"The story had George flirting with a chorus girl, and Marian finds out about it. She is just furious with him. The show opens with pillows and bed sheets flying and hitting George. Finally, Marian appears, and tells George he can sleep wherever he likes as long as it's not with her. George says 'You can't shut me out, we're married.' Marian says, 'We're not married anymore. Remember our wedding vows? Until death do us part?' At the end of the program, George proposes to her all over again complete with candy and flowers. That was a cute episode, and one of my favorites."

One humorous (but at the time, distressing) experience Anne remembers from the show concerns the Kirbys' St. Bernard, Neil, who weighed an imposing 165 pounds. He was the ghostly dog who delighted audiences with his penchant for drinking brandy out of a large snifter.

"We had to shoot a commercial for Camel cigarettes. At that time, I was pregnant. I didn't tell anyone because I didn't want to be fussed over. I didn't want the producers to worry because Robert and I had it timed so that I could have our child on hiatus. In those days, we wore the big poodle skirts. I didn't gain much weight anyway. I only gained ten pounds.

"This commercial necessitated our riding in a roller coaster. The dog sat in between Robert and me. He was a wonderful dog—but he was huge and very wet-mouthed. He'd shake his head, and could hit you from twenty feet away with that saliva. It's early in the morning. I'm not feeling too well with my pregnancy anyway. Having to ride on that roller coaster first thing in the morning, with that dog with his halitosis sitting between us, is one of the most trying experiences I can remember. I kept thinking 'I'll never make it, I'll never make it!' It would have been wonderful," she says, cringing at the memory, "if I had gotten sick on the side of the roller coaster during the filming of the commercial. I held on and didn't (get sick). It was funny in a way. When I look back at it now, I can laugh."

Anne was expecting her eldest son, Jeffreys Sterling ("The last time I got first billing in the family," chuckles Anne), during the commercial incident. The Sterlings' other two sons are Robert Dana Sterling (called Dana to avoid the confusion of too many Roberts) and Tyler Marcus Sterling.

Robert Sterling, Neil the St. Bernard, and Anne Jeffreys in the pilot episode of *Topper*, in which the Kirbys become merry ghosts following an avalanche.

"Our third son was a slip-up," laughs Anne. "On a trip to Spain, we took a siesta like everyone else, and Tyler was conceived. He was born just fourteen months after Dana, so your plans don't always go as they're supposed to. But he's a love. All my children are wonderful. I adore them. I also have three grandchildren," she adds with pride.

The Sterling sons did not follow their parents' footsteps into show business careers. "Robert didn't want them to act. He feels that it's a tough business for a man. All three appeared with me in shows on stage, so they can't say they weren't allowed to act. They all ended up standing out in different things. Jeff is a business entrepreneur, Tyler is in the construction business and is also a painter, and Dana must be near the sea. He's a sailor, totally involved with his boats."

For all intensive purposes, Robert Sterling has retired from the acting profession. A couple of experiences with his last two series, *Love That Jill* and *Ichabod and Me*, were less than pleasant and led to his retirement.

"We got into big altercations about how the scripts were going on *Love That Jill*. They started out very good ... slick and well written," remembers Anne. "Then they became slapstick, incomprehensible and stupid, really. Finally, after we did the twelfth show, we went to Hal Roach, the head of the studio at the time, and expressed our unhappiness. He expressed his unhappiness, and we said, 'Why don't we just call it quits.' Actually, Robert said, 'I'm not doing this thirteenth one, it's too stupid to be believed.'

"After the 'Jill' series, Robert did a series called *Ichabod and Me*. He just hated it. He'd get up in the morning and say, 'God, I'd give anything not to have to do this crap.' It was torture for him. When he finished that last series, he said, 'That's it. I'm getting out of this business!' He decided to go into the computer business for a while, and also went into making custom-made golf clubs called Sterling Clubs. At the moment, he's retired. He enjoys playing golf with his buddies at the country club.

"I have been able to get him, every once in a while, to do a guest shot with me. He would almost always say, 'No, absolutely not!' I did blackmail him into doing a couple of them with me," continues Anne with a laugh. "We enjoyed doing *Murder She Wrote*. We both like Angela Lansbury very much. I love to have him acting with me again. I miss his company on the set ... and riding to work with him, sharing the same joys and problems. It's togetherness that I've enjoyed with my husband over the years. It's been very easy ... our marriage has just worked. We have respect for each other. We share a good sense of humor and laugh at a lot of things together. It's worked out quite, quite nicely."

Since 1984, Anne has had a recurring role in the daytime drama *General Hospital*. It's split evenly down the middle: If she's not recognized as "Marian Kirby" by fans, she's recognized for her role on the widely watched soap opera. Jeffreys also devotes her time to charitable endeavors such as Child Help USA, SHARE, and the Society for Singers.

"Robert doesn't always like to go to all the dinners and charitable functions that I attend," says Anne. "He's an avid reader. He just devours books. I have various friends take me to these events. Quite often it's Cesar Romero, who is an old family friend. Cesar will come to pick me up, and he and Robert will sit down and talk while I finish dressing. Robert sees us off at the door and says, 'Have a good time.' He then puts a book under his arm and goes happily back to his room to read," laughs Anne. "Cesar is just like I am. He likes to go, go, go! He's a lovely gentleman . . . he really is."

Anne is also in business with her own jewelry line of pink and gold rubies called Ruby Blues, and is a matinee hostess for the cable station American Movie Classics.

"I was so pleased when they asked me to be a hostess on AMC. Television today has changed. I just can't find anything I want to watch with the exception of classic films. I'm tired of all the sex and violence. I want them to go back to romantic stories . . . fantasies. We live in a real world. Why do we have to take that as our entertainment?"

Why, indeed—a perceptive question from an actress who has brought joy to audiences everywhere with romance, fantasy, and most of all, quality entertainment. As long as *Topper* comes back in reruns periodically, there will still be a glimmer of romance and fantasy in our lives.

Meredith MacRae

Series: *My Three Sons*
Role: Sally Ann Morrison Douglas (1963–1965)
Series: *Petticoat Junction*
Role: Billie Jo Bradley (1966–1970)

Meredith MacRae may have been born into the limelight of the entertainment industry as the daughter of Gordon and Sheila MacRae; however, she has succeeded on her own as a triple threat — actress, producer and Emmy Award–winning television interviewer. A dark-eyed, blonde beauty with an appealing, slightly husky voice, Meredith is a strong woman who has never been content to take the easy road and readily accepts career challenges. When she first started in the business, she never traded on her family's name, even though it would have made things easier for her. As a producer and interviewer today, she will choose the controversial subject or interview rather than the comfortable one.

Meredith made her film debut at the age of seven in *By the Light of the Silvery Moon,* a light-hearted musical which starred her father and Doris Day.

"Ever since I could remember, I've always wanted to be in show business. I never, ever considered anything else," says Meredith. "I just loved the business. It was so much a part of my life. It wasn't any big decision or anything . . . it was just sort of by osmosis, I guess. I started appearing as an extra in a couple of my dad's films. I would also get up on stage with him whenever I had a chance. I was a real ham," she adds with a laugh.

Her parents had mixed feelings about their daughter venturing into the tough world of show business.

"They were really sort of ambivalent," recalls Meredith. "On the one hand, I wanted to be in the business when I was very young. I had the opportunity once to star in a television series as a kid. They wouldn't let me. They said, 'We absolutely refuse. You have to finish high school and have a year of college, and then if you want to quit your education . . . you can.' I was an A student, and they really thought it would be wrong for me to

Meredith MacRae

do the series. I think they were right. After that, they let it be my own decision . . . they didn't encourage me and they didn't discourage me. They
figured that I should do what I wanted, which is the way I'm going to be
with my daughter. In a way, I hope that she doesn't go into our business.
I think it's a terribly difficult business. But if she chooses to—then that's
fine. I'm certainly not going to encourage her."

Allison, MacRae's daughter from her eighteen-year marriage to actor
Greg Mullavey, was born in 1974, and she wants to be a producer like her
mother. "She dances and she acts. Although she says she wants to produce, I think the ham in her will probably emerge once again," laughs
Meredith, "and she'll probably want to be a performer."

Meredith wasn't much older than her daughter is now when she received her first regular role on a television series. She played Mike's girl-friend Sally on the long-running hit situation comedy *My Three Sons*.

"I tried out for parts for a whole year and didn't get any roles at all. All of a sudden, I got a couple at once," recalls Meredith. "I got *My Three Sons* and another movie. I read for it and tested with a couple of other girls. It's funny because my dad used to love to tell this story. Shortly after I joined the cast of the show, my father was playing golf with Don Fedderson, who was the producer of *My Three Sons*. My father said, 'Gee, how is my little daughter working out?' and Don said, 'Who is your daughter?' And my dad said, 'Meredith MacRae is my daughter.' Don had no idea that I was Gordon MacRae's daughter. My dad was really proud because I got the part on my own with no nepotism and no parental phone calls. I just read, and they liked my reading and the quality I had and that was that."

Mike, who was played by Tim Considine, was the eldest son of Fred MacMurray on *My Three Sons*, and the first to get married . . . to Meredith's character. The show switched from black and white to color, and changed networks from ABC to CBS, in September of 1965. Unfortunately, the two characters of Mike and Sally were never heard from again on the show after the wedding. Considine left the show, and Meredith's character went with him.

It's interesting and rather disconcerting that beloved characters in family sitcoms often "leave town" and promptly drop off the face of the earth. They're just not ever mentioned again. It's as if they never existed in the first place — which would make a good *Twilight Zone* episode, but doesn't go along with the premise of a family show where viewers have watched characters and grown close to them over the years.

Until recently, the black and white episodes of *My Three Sons* were never shown in syndication. For the past several years, the popular cable station Nickelodeon has been running them. Many people, including the actors themselves, are seeing the shows again for the first time in years. How does Meredith feel when she sees the shows now?

"Oh, very nostalgic and very warm. It was just a wonderful way to break into the business. I mean it was great to work with some of the finest actors ever, like Fred MacMurray and William Frawley. Tim Considine, Don Grady, and Stanley and Barry Livingston were all like a family to me. The set was just like having a second home, and I loved it."

Meredith says she has seen Tim Considine on occasion over the years, after their roles on *My Three Sons* ended. Considine has since become a TV writer and director.

Much of the time during the fifties and early sixties, television portrayals of teenage girls were more than just a little bit on the bubble-headed side. McRae's portrayal of Sally was cool and mature for one so young.

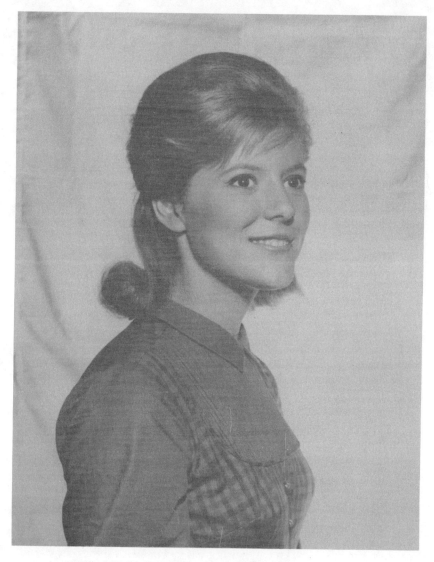

Meredith MacRae as she appeared on *My Three Sons*.

These were elements she also brought to her role as the eldest sister, Billie Jo Bradley, on *Petticoat Junction*. Meredith's Billie Jo was elegant, level-headed and the wisest of the sisters.

Billie Jo was the sister who started a women's liberation movement in Hooterville in the episode "Susan B. Anthony, I Love You," and brought sensitivity training to the small rural town in "Love Rears Its Ugly Head."

A 1966 cast shot from *Petticoat Junction:* Lori Saunders, Linda Kaye Henning and Meredith MacRae.

Meredith was the fourth actress to take over the role, if you count Sharon Tate, who played the part in the pilot. Jeannine Riley and Gunilla Hutton were the two actresses who preceded Meredith as Billie Jo. MacRae also held on to the role the longest — for four years — and is the one best remembered by many as the knockout blonde sister.

Interestingly, television audiences across the country watched both mother and daughter every week (on Saturday nights) for the same time period of four years (1966–1970) — Meredith on *Petticoat Junction* and her mother, Sheila MacRae, on the *Jackie Gleason Show.* Sheila played Alice Kramden in the "Honeymooners" portion of the program.

MacRae has some very fond memories of her *Petticoat Junction* days.

"Those were fun times," reflects Meredith. "On the set, Edgar Buchanan (Uncle Joe Carson) was just a riot. He would tell these wonderful jokes, and he had you laughing all the time. He was just delightful.

"Also, we girls were always doing things together. We decided we were all going to learn how to hook rugs because there was a lot of time sitting around between scenes. We'd sometimes have hours between scenes. So we would sit around, and we were hooking these rugs. We used to kid around and call ourselves 'The Three Hookers,'" laughs Meredith. "I'm the only one who didn't finish my rug—the other two girls got their rugs done.

"I'd say the most fun we had, though, was when we'd go on tour. I mean the show was an absolute smash during the time that I was on it. We went on *The Tonight Show*, and we had a musical act we did. We did personal appearances, nightclubs, circuses and state fairs. We wore these matching mini-dresses and matching go-go boots. We had a lot of fun traveling around the country, mostly on weekends and sometimes during the show's hiatus. We had a ball. We'd order room service, stay up late, talk, and work. It was just a lot of fun.

"I remember once we played the Steel Pier in Atlantic City. We had been on tour for a long time. This was our last job, and then we'd start filming the show again. So, we knew that we wouldn't have to go out and do more personal appearances for at least six months. By the end of this tour, our boots were just disgusting. They were scuffed, dirty and smelly. So, we decided after the midnight show, we would all take our boots and throw them over the Steel Pier into the Atlantic Ocean. And that's just what we did," laughs Meredith.

MacRae also recalled a story that's not so funny from that same trip to the Steel Pier.

"There was this little chicken in the amusement arcade. It was billed as the Dancing Chicken. They had no water for him in his cage. We went in and complained. And the next time we went back, they were taking a little better care of him—at least he had water.

"On *Petticoat Junction*, we just had a lot of fun. We were young, in our early twenties. We just laughed, gossiped and did what girls do when they get together. There was no dissension on the set—it was not like *Designing Women*. We all got along well. It was another family for me, and I loved it very much."

MacRae has kept in close touch with her co-stars Lori Saunders (Bobbie Jo) and Linda Kaye Henning (Betty Jo) over the years. MacRae and Henning were producing partners for a reunion show called *Hello Again, Hooterville* (which unfortunately did not come about because of red tape concerning film clip rights) as well as other projects, including one for a Pulitzer Prize–winning novel.

"Linda Henning and I are still very close friends. We went to school together at UCLA both during and after *Petticoat Junction*. I consider her one of my very good friends. We had lunch last week, and dinner the week before. We keep in touch a lot. I see Lori Saunders about once a year. She lives up in Santa Barbara, so I don't see her as often. Lori and I were actually really close during the show, and after the show Linda and I became closer because we were business partners as well as friends."

During the 1980s, Meredith hosted a local Los Angeles talk show, *Mid–Morning L.A.*, for which she won an Emmy Award. Since then she has done countless interviews, and has been heavily involved in producing.

"I've always loved the intelllectual side of the business," explains MacRae. "As an actress—as much as I enjoy acting—you have very little power of control. As a producer you have a lot of control, which I love. You're the one who decides what questions to ask. I write all of my own questions. You can shape the interview in the way you'd like it to go or not. You have a lot of power and control. I like the controversial interview. That's why I'd like to interview G. Gordon Liddy as opposed to just a straight TV or movie star interview, because a lot of times actors are more private. They're tired of people prying into their lives, and they don't reveal as much."

MacRae's most recent project is her syndicated television show *Born Famous*. She produces the show as well as doing the interviews, which feature other children of celebrities. Since no one knows better than she what it is like to be "born famous," Meredith thought it would be interesting to compare notes with people who grew up in similar circumstances.

"Basically, I just felt that we grow up totally different than the average person. First of all, you grow up surrounded by a lot of glamour. And you live in an unreal world of glitter. Your 'aunts' and 'uncles' are Aunt Lucy (Ball), Uncle Desi (Arnaz), and then there's Aunt Doris (Day), and Uncle Dean (Martin)—so you grow up with a lot of famous people and you get used to them. I also felt it would be interesting to talk about the pluses and minuses, the advantages and disadvantages, with others who had been through the same experience.

"We all learned early that we had to share our parents with the public. My worst childhood memory was when my dad was arrested for drunken driving. It made the *Los Angeles Times*. The next day in school I felt that all the kids were making fun of me. They never would have known if my dad hadn't been famous."

Meredith is also much in demand as a public speaker. She talks about everything from career networking for women to alcoholism. Her father, Gordon MacRae, was an alcoholic who eventually got help for his disease. He spent many of the years before his death in 1986 in recovery, dedicated to helping others. He was on the board of the National Council on Alcoholism. After his death, Meredith took over his position on the board.

"The first time I had been asked to give a speech on the subject of alcoholism, my father was still alive," explains Meredith. "He happened to be visiting me and staying with me. I asked my dad how he felt about my speaking publicly about our family and alcoholism. He said that he liked the idea, because by this time he was sober. He had been going around the country giving a lot of speeches. He thought it was good for me to do it from my perspective."

One of the most personally rewarding projects for MacRae was her award-winning special *A Second Chance: Surviving Alcoholism*. It was an overview of alcoholism, which is difficult to do in forty-two minutes, says Meredith. "I was really proud of that show. It's also very rewarding when I give speeches on alcoholism. Sometimes my favorite part is after the speech when people tell me that I've reached them."

Meredith also has initiated several women's support groups. "One group gets together once a month. We've been getting together since 1979. We've had everything in the group happen from children ending up in jail, to husbands who have been on drugs. I mean just about every single problem you can think of has surfaced at one time or another.

"I have another group called 'Fun Night' where I invite a different group of women out every couple of months to just go out and have fun. I don't think we have enough fun in our lives. Sometimes we even need to program in fun. But just getting through life . . . I think we need to help one another. It's nice to be able to have other women to share with. There's nothing like having a good woman friend or a group of women friends."

Since her divorce, Meredith has been raising her teenage daughter as a single mother. MacRae loves traveling, and takes her daughter with her whenever possible. Already in her young life, Allison has experienced Europe, Bangkok and El Salvador. Meredith says she finds that listening is very important when raising a teenager.

"Listen as much as you can and judge as little as possible," she advises. "I'm learning my way with Allison. If she feels that I am being judgmental and critical, she is not going to share with me and open up during the times when I will really want her to open up. We have good lines of communication. We do argue sometimes, but that's normal. I definitely plan some time for just the two of us, whether it's going to a movie, shopping or to a game. I also think it's important to set limits and boundaries."

Limits and boundaries won't apply to Meredith MacRae's future. She would like to continue acting, hosting, interviewing and producing. With her unique combination of a warm on-camera style and a penchant for hard-hitting subjects and controversy, there are limitless possibilites and bound to be a few surprises in store for viewers.

Julie Newmar

Series: *My Living Doll*
Role: Rhoda Miller (The Robot) (1964–1965)
Series: *Batman*
Role: The Catwoman (1966–1967)

While many undoubtedly think of Julie Newmar as one of television's great beauties, she is also an excellent comedienne whose humor shines through in her unique characterizations.

Newmar brought more than just a beautiful face and dynamite figure to the role of Catwoman on the satirical fantasy series *Batman*. Her playful qualities have made her the most memorable actress to play the role. You couldn't possibly hate Julie's comic villainess — you have to love her. Newmar gave Catwoman an exuberance and vivacity that no other actress could equal. As Alan Napier (Alfred on *Batman*) once pointed out, "Julie Newmar was the best Catwoman . . . the only Catwoman."

Statuesque, with tumbling chestnut hair and almond-shaped brown eyes, this actress, best known for her supernatural roles, began her career in the arts through music. She graduated high school at the tender age of fifteen. Immediately thereafter she became a prima ballerina for the Los Angeles Opera.

"I was at least five when I began to study ballet. Music was introduced into my life very early. I was quite a good pianist and studied music for many years. So music was a precursor to dancing, because dancing is music," Newmar points out.

Julie Newmar is the daughter of an entertainer (her mother, Helen Jesmer, was in the *Follies of 1920*) and a college professor (Donald Newmeyer).

"My mother encouraged my interest in dance. My father was once a great football player, so I suppose that introduced the element of athletics which through my mother became dance. I have probably danced every form of dance that there is," she says with a giggle. "I was even a flamenco dancer at the age of fifteen, which is the normal age for flamenco

83

Julie Newmar

dancers. I also did Balinese dance, but ballet dance is my true love. I still dance ballet."

As a little girl, Julie idolized Rita Hayworth and even studied dance with Hayworth's father, Eduardo Cansino.

"Rita Hayworth had a great influence on me, on my life. There was a photograph of me in the *New York Daily News* about a month ago, and

I treasure it. I won't take it off my shelf because I resemble Rita Hayworth in it," laughs Julie. "I tried to fix my hair like hers and even tried to manicure my nails like hers. We all do that as kids.

"She was the one and only queen of the silver screen. She had passion. And in those days they had such beautiful diction. They looked like ladies, and behaved in public in a glorious way. The stars dressed well. We don't do that anymore and it's noticeable. It's missed. I miss that in society. I miss those qualities. I miss people who speak well because it's more loving. You don't want to talk like this," she says in a horribly squeaky voice. "Doesn't that hurt your ears? People actually talk like that, and they're on the movie screens! I won't pay for that kind of insult in my ears."

Newmar never did get to meet Rita Hayworth.

"You almost don't want to meet your heroines. It might spoil the illusion. It was all right for me not to meet her. I wanted to keep her as a dream image, so that seemed okay."

At the beginning of her career, one of Newmar's first jobs was as a dancer and choreographer at Universal Studios. At the age of nineteen, she also taught dance.

"I remember actually holding dance classes for a number of the stars. They used to have a system at Universal Studios where they had a series of bungalows on the lot. There they would give acting, singing and dancing lessons. I used to teach dance for every century," she laughs. "I remember dancing-in for Yvonne DeCarlo and Suzan Ball. 'Dancing-in' means that in camera shots far from the camera, where they can't see your face, a dancer dances for the star. A dance-in is a double with more talent!"

Acting came along for Newmar later, in New York, after she'd already reached Broadway as a dancer.

"It seemed a natural transition after I'd reached Broadway and done muscials like *Silk Stockings* by Cole Porter," reflects Julie, who also made quite an impression as Stupefyin' Jones in *Li'l Abner*. "Someone saw a poster of me wearing my *Li'l Abner* costume, which stood seven or eight feet high outside of the St. James Theater. They said, 'She'd make a great Swede.' And lo and behold, I am a Swede, at least one-quarter Swedish from my grandmother. And that's how the part of Katrin in *Marriage-Go-Round* came about."

Newmar's portrayal of the sexy Swedish bombshell who wants a happily married but very tempted middle-aged man to father her baby (and almost breaks up his marriage in the process) garnered her a Tony Award for Best Supporting Actress.

"Charles Boyer had it in his contract that he would have to okay any actress that played the part. Thank God, I was only an inch or two taller than him," laughs the 5' 11" actress. "I remember doing the whole play on

Broadway in flats! If you lean a certain way you can appear to be shorter than your leading man, and that was important in those days! You don't have to worry about that anymore."

Newmar loved the role in *Marriage-Go-Round*. "I had the advantage of working with two of the most superb performers," she says of Charles Boyer and Claudette Colbert. "Boy, was I going to pick up things there, obviously. I mean, you're flying high when performing with people of that caliber."

Julie also played Katrin in the film *Marriage-Go-Round* a couple of years after playing the role on Broadway. In the 1960 film version, the married couple were portrayed by James Mason and Susan Hayward.

Newmar remembers, "Susan Hayward kept very much to herself. I never got to know her. But she turned in a fine performance. James Mason was the most giving actor, the most generous man, and kindest performer. He was perhaps my all-time favorite because of his generosity . . . his humanness. If you happened to be in the wrong camera light, he would help you, ever so gently, to make it better for *you*. He didn't show off by doing it. He didn't help you to make himself look better to others — he gave it to you out of pure generosity. Being a real actor, rather than a pretty boy, I think he made the higher choice. He was a great man.

"The only thing is that the film lacks the edge, the champagne quality that it had on the stage. And that's because during those times the studios kept a lot of directors and certain people under contract. And so they would hire the people who were under contract regardless of whether they were right to do the particular vehicle."

In general, as an actress, Newmar prefers stage to film work.

"There's a wonderful thing about theater — you do a play from beginning to end. In the movies, you do it in the middle, then you do the end, then you go back and pick something up three months later. And everybody else has control of your act in film. I've seen things I've done, and have just been horrified at what they did with what I gave them. Some of the people in charge don't have the wisdom to select what's great or what's powerful or what's big and important. They go for the lower dimension . . . the lower choice."

Newmar, a very funny woman in real life as well as a marvelous comedienne in performance, believes in the healing powers of comedy.

"Comedy is about pain. You never want to leave an audience with pain. Drama is about pain. You want to be able to get that pain up and out. And that's an act of genius that some people are born with and others learn. Some actors never get it. But it is a great, great, immeasurable gift when you can make someone laugh because it is in essence quite healing," says Julie earnestly.

"That's why half-hour situation comedies are good for people. I mean here are these actors, acting out things that might be happening in your lifetime or you see these things happening to your neighbor — and they act it out for you for free. They're doing it for you. If the story is told well, it influences you to make the higher choice if a situation arises in your own life. I think that's why situation comedies have so much popularity — because of the release. They relieve people of life's dilemmas and the quandaries we all get into."

An early television role for Newmar was in "Of Late, I Think of Cliffordville," a classic two-part episode of the *Twilight Zone* series. Julie played the devil, who was called Miss Devlin. Clad in a business suit, with blond hair and two cute little horns sticking out on the top of her head, Newmar as Miss Devlin was a master negotiator. Her wicked laugh and the mischievous gleam in her eye were hints of traits that Julie would later put into Catwoman. And like all Newmar's characterizations, even though the character was a devil, you still had to like her. The man with whom Miss Devlin negotiated deserved what he had coming.

Newmar's first television series role was as Rhoda the Robot on *My Living Doll*, which also starred Bob Cummings as Dr. Bob McDonald, the scientist who invented Robot AF709. Rhoda often malfunctioned mechanically and would show this by acting inebriated or dizzy. She was supposed to be a psychiatric patient, which to some extent explained her strange behavior to those around her (who, of course, didn't know she was a robot). Rhoda was controlled by beauty marks on her back (they were her buttons).

"That role was a great challenge," says Julie. "How do you interest an audience in a piece of machinery? I mean, I usually kick the damn things when they aren't working. I swear and curse and call someone in and say, 'Here, you fix it!' How do you make yourself interesting as a robot? You can act like a piece of machinery, have bent elbows and a crooked walk and that sort of thing. But how do you have a soul when you're a machine? It took me thirteen weeks before I could say I owned the role. It took me that long. It was hugely challenging. And I liked my work in that show. At the time, I was quite a serious actress. I had just graduated from the Actors Studio."

Unfortunately *My Living Doll* will never be shown in reruns. With sixties fantasy shows doing so well in syndication, *My Living Doll* would surely have been a welcome addition to the genre.

"They burned it," says Julie sadly. "They burned all the original tapes, they're all gone. CBS didn't have a place to store them."

Even though we don't have Julie's Rhoda the Robot to watch, we will fortunately have Catwoman in syndication indefinitely.

Newmar relishes her comic portrayal of the villainess, bringing her dancer's grace to the feline character. Her physical movements and the

Bob Cummings and Julie Newmar in *My Living Doll*.

sounds she makes are subtly catlike. Whether she's swinging on her swing, swatting at a ball of yarn or reclining seductively while planning her next caper, she seems to be completely amused by all around her as well as having non-stop fun.

   The Catwoman character started off a little more evil than she ended up. In the beginning, she wasn't portrayed quite as much in love with

Newmar as Catwoman, plotting her next crime on her meowing cat phone in *Batman*.

Batman as she was towards the end of Newmar's six episodes. The character was softened a bit.

There's no question that Catwoman had a thing for Batman. She thought of him as a sex object. In a funny scene in the "Cat's Meow" episode, Catwoman has Batman trapped in an echo torture chamber where sounds will be magnified 10,000,000 times. Catwoman says to Batman,

"Your brains will be turned to mush. Then I shall return and you will be mine forever, Batman. We will have to sacrifice your intellect, but with a build like yours, who cares. After all, one can't have her cake and eat it too."

Catwoman was also not above using her feminine wiles to trick Batman. She would pretend to be subservient, cry or say, "Please let me powder my nose before you send me up the river," and then she'd do something like stick her claws out and zap him with a brightly colored poisonous gas. Newmar was hilarious in these scenes.

Stanley Ralph Ross wrote all of the Catwoman episodes of *Batman* with the exception of "The Sandman Cometh, the Catwoman Goeth." Every episode that featured Catwoman as the sole villain was brilliantly written by Ross.

"Bless his sweet life," sighs Julie. "He wrote the best character for me. I've been in love with that man for more than twenty years! He wrote five of the six episodes which were just works of art."

Newmar remembers that the period before she filmed her first episode of *Batman* was rather rushed.

"They called me on a Friday. I flew in on Sunday from New York City, and on Monday I was getting measured for my costume," recalls Julie, referring to that famous, skin-tight black costume, which, draped around Newmar, sends men into a tailspin. "Tuesday morning I was on the set. It was push, push, push. I'm very meticulous about my work. I like to be more than prepared because there's a certain nervousness and tension when all the scenes are yours on a certain day. If you looked at my scripts you'd see what looks like chicken marks all over every page," she continues, explaining about her notes. "And sometimes, if I think they'll ever be found, I'll write them out in a kind of secret script, so only I know what the notes mean.

"It's called the sub-text. One writes the sub-text to the actual dialogue. One says the actual dialogue but thinks in one's mind the sub-text so that the experience of your own life and writer's words blend together. It takes enormous concentration. At least that's the way I work. I'm not a fast study. But I am very quick to comprehend what scenes are about. It's kind of like a piece of sculpture. I sit with it in my lap for a long time, for many days and nights. I hear it in my head like music. For instance, there are so many beats for certain scenes. To me, the sub-text is very important. You see, if I know what the author intended, what the director would like, and how it would help the totality of the story—then I can write a powerful sub-text. And that's really what's coming across on screen the sub-text. Stanley's words and my sub-text," she adds with a laugh.

"Catwoman is one of the most desirable female roles in the history of performing. Women have gone through a lot of dos and don'ts, shoulds and shouldn'ts, pinched waists, flat breasts and every sort of dimension of female behavior. It has all been imposed as well as self-imposed on women. And yet, the Catwoman is forever," says Julie.

Men love Newmar's Catwoman character because of her sensuality and beauty, and women would like to be more like her—independent and in charge. Everyone—man, woman and child—loves her humor.

"I think people would like to be more like Catwoman because there's so much *enthusiance* in her." ("I constantly use that word because it's just a great word," she says of the term she created.) "I think the Catwoman is laughing all the time. She's always having a goood time. Now, I am Julie Newmar, and I am always having a wonderful time. Even if I were going to kill you in a film, I'd still be having a good time," laughs Julie. "Catwoman has a sense of life that people envy and wish that they had. It's a sense of fun. No matter what happens, a cat lands on its four feet. It's not going to land on its neck, it's not going to land on its tail. It's going to land on its feet. And it will never run away, it will saunter off with its tail in the air and its ass in your face. They're just unbelievable, cats! Think of it, they're incredible creatures."

Newmar also believes that Catwoman should be played by someone who is not too young. "She should be played by someone twenty-six to thirty-four. It takes wisdom, so the actress shouldn't be too young. But she must be powerfully, physically strong."

Julie remembers the set of *Batman* with great fondness.

"It was a good, ebullient and strong set—easygoing but not easy off. I mean, they were in charge. Things happened very quickly. And there was a great sense of the total picture in all the gifts of the various people from the writers, producer and art designer to the camera man and director. They made an all-time classic. It just clicked."

Newmar still gets together with her *Batman* co-stars at various reunions and conventions.

"The show is still so popular. From time to time, I see both Burt Ward and Adam West. It's lots of fun, and we laugh. We ride around in limousines wherever we're going. We tell tales and we're just as silly as we used to be. Gosh, it's great! I guess for the most part we haven't changed very much. Good or bad, we're all still the same," laughs Julie.

When asked for a theory on why she is often cast in supernatural roles, such as devils, robots, and even Mother Nature on Dutch Masters cigar commercials, Newmar says, "Supernatural? I guess I am a bit larger than life. Just a bit."

Today, Julie Newmar is involved in her own real estate business, and has a patent pending for "Nudemar" pantyhose, which she says are more flattering to women's figures. She works out of a home office so she can be close by for her young son.

"It's so much fun. I love being a parent and having a family. I love my house and garden and kitchen—all the domesticity," muses Julie.

"With wisdom and intelligence, social life is really for the young. I don't need that late night stuff, all those parties, it zaps your energy. I'd much rather work seventy hours a week and be highly productive. I don't need anyone's opinion anymore. I don't care what people think. I'm way beyond that. I never clamor for publicity, people call me up.

"There is great value in being able to change," she continues. "I feel I've lived three or four lifetimes already. I'm very healthy. A lot of people don't make it in a healthy way through life. And, I think, allowing change can improve the health. If we stay frozen with our ideas, concepts and attitudes—that's like dying.

"I think the bottom line in life is to enjoy it. In orchestra you tune your instrument slightly sweet. In other words, the 'A' may be 1/50th sharp rather than flat. So tune your life to the sweet. People will try to run you over, but stand up for yourself. And you'll be more powerful if you're knocked down. But for God's sake, stand up and laugh."

Gary Owens

Series: *McHale's Navy*
Recurring role as a war correspondent (1963–1966)
Series: *The Green Hornet*
Series: *Rowan & Martin's Laugh-In* (1966–1967)
Role: Regular (1968–1973)

There is no better example of a modern-day Renaissance man than Gary Owens. While he is most famous for his hand-cupped-over-the-ear, exaggerated announcer character on *Rowan & Martin's Laugh-In*, Owens is also an erudite author, a successful businessman, a cartoonist and a popular radio personality—not to mention a marvelous comedian.

Long before Steve Martin put an arrow through his head doing "wild and crazy" comedy routines, audiences had the conservatively dressed, seemingly serious Gary Owens spoofing the news, horoscopes, soap operas and commercials with his rich baritone voice and his own brand of zaniness.

This warm and genial entertainer will often pepper his conversation with hilarious observations. Unlike many comedians who are shy and rather serious in real life, Owens is a truly funny man both off and on stage.

Gary Owens was born in Mitchell, South Dakota. His father was a sheriff and his mother the county auditor and treasurer.

"My sister owns a newspaper," adds Gary. "She has always been a very literary person. As a matter of fact, we've always had a lot of literary people in our family. I had several uncles who owned newspapers. Marcus Childs, who won the Pulitzer Prize twenty-five or thirty years ago, is a relative. That's kind of my background . . . newspapering."

A syndicated newspaper columnist and author of several books, he is currently working on a comedy book entitled "A Gary Owens Chrestomathy." *Chrestomathy* is a word H.L. Mencken used to describe a collection of his articles, says Gary.

An avid reader, Owens has more than 10,000 books in his own personal library. "I've always loved a big library. I have, I don't know how many hundreds of just quotation books. The fact that anyone has a love for a library now may be a little archaic, because everything is computerized. But there is a love for books alone . . . just the feeling and texture of a book," he adds.

His first endeavor in the creative world was when he was just twelve years old. Gary was one of the few people who actually won an art scholarship from one of those "Draw Me and Win an Art Scholarship" advertisements. One of the ways in which he worked his way through college was by drawing freelance for various "gag" magazines.

"I won an art scholarship from Minneapolis Art Instruction. The man who chose my drawings was Charlie Schultz, who created "Peanuts" later on. That was the start of cartooning for me. I still love it. I'm still a member of the National Cartoonists Society," says Gary with pride. "I think Carol Burnett and I are the only two show business people who are members but don't make a living drawing cartoons. I'm getting some drawings ready for a showing next year. My work is more like the illustration boards that were on cartoon/comic strips. Cartooning was definitely my first love."

At the age of sixteen, when most people are worrying about teenage concerns like grades and dates, Owens was already well on his way with his various careers.

"I started in radio as a substitute newscaster doing summer vacation relief back in South Dakota. Tom Brokaw and I are from the same area. Tom started two years after I did," recalls Gary. "Suddenly, the man whose place I was taking wired us from his vacation in California saying that he wouldn't be returning. So it opened up a job for me. I ended up becoming a teenage news director. At the age of sixteen, I had the job of a man who was probably thirty-five at the time.

"So I would go to college in the morning from 8 a.m. until noon, and work at the radio station from noon until 10:30 in the evening. Then I'd scamper off across the street to the newspaper, *The Daily Republic*, where I was a sportswriter and cartoonist," continues Gary, remembering his hectic schedule.

One of Owens' funniest stories regarding radio comes from a period of time that he spent as a disc jockey in Denver, Colorado.

"A very good friend of mine, Perry Allen, was still a bachelor who would come in at strange hours. He did a radio show in the afternoon on a competing station. We had a 'Gary Owens Frankenstein Screaming Contest,' and it was connected with a recording machine. What the caller would do is give his name, address and then scream at the top of his lungs. The people with the ten best screams would win a prize. Well, this special scream-line number was only one digit different than Perry Allen's home number. Perry was my best friend, and I was used to calling him every day. By accident, I gave out his home phone number on the air. So here's a guy

Gary Owens

who comes in at four in the morning. At six in the morning—suddenly—not one but 200 people start calling him saying, 'Hello, my name is Fred Nernie, AAARGH!'

"He has no idea what's going on. I mean why are these people calling him, giving their names and screaming their heads off?" laughs Gary. "He wouldn't talk to me for a month after that. I didn't do it purposely, it was just one of those things where I accidentally gave out the wrong number."

Owens, who was named "The Babe Ruth of Broadcasting" by *Radio and Records*, moved to Los Angeles in 1960 and promptly found work in both radio and television. From 1962 until 1982, he had his own show on Gene Autry's Los Angeles radio station, KMPC. Owens also had a national radio show which was broadcast simultaneously on 500 stations around the world.

During the early sixties, Owens began doing voice-overs for cartoons. To date, Gary says he's done more than 1500 cartoons and an amazing 1000 television shows.

One of his first television roles was on *The Jack Benny Show*. He played Jack's secretary's boyfriend on a couple of episodes. "I was just a young man," he remembers, "and Jack was very kind to me."

Some of his pre–*Laugh-In* television guest spots include a couple of episodes of *The Munsters*, and regular roles on *McHale's Navy* and *The Green Hornet*. One of his most memorable guest shots was on a very funny episode of *I Dream of Jeannie* which had Jeannie auditioning for Gary in hopes of getting a role on *Laugh-In*. Owens was also the announcer for *The Wonderful World of Disney* and *Bewitched* for many years.

George Schlatter, the producer of *Rowan & Martin's Laugh-In*, used to listen to Owens on the radio, and was impresed by Gary's novel comedic style. Schlatter hired Owens without an audition for *Laugh-In*, but wasn't sure exactly what role he would play on the show.

"George, Digby Wolfe, Arte Johnson and I went out to lunch at the Smoke House Restaurant in Burbank. We had typewriter goop all over our hands because we'd been writing bad jokes all morning in the office across the street," remembers Gary with a smile. "George and I went to the restroom to wash our hands. Then everybody came into the restroom. It was an old tile bathroom and as I got in there, I just put my hand over my ear to satirize the old radio announcers, who were too vain to wear ear phones, because it might have removed their toupees or something. Anyway, I put my hand over my ear and said, 'My, the acoustics are good in here.' George said, 'That's it! That's what I want you to do on the show!' And I said, 'Do what? Wash my hands?' and he said, 'No, be the announcer who is from another dimension . . . an old announcer who is not with it because of the tumult that's going on around him.' And that's how it all began. I remember *The Hollywood Reporter* said, 'Laugh-In Comic Signed in Men's Restroom in Burbank!'" he laughs.

Owens also recounted the story of how Henry Gibson got his job on *Laugh-In*.

"George Schlatter was very busy. He had both phones going at all times. Henry came into George's office and sat down. He waited there

Owens and *Laugh-In* co-star Goldie Hawn.

patiently for about forty-five minutes. George hadn't even acknowledged him, he was so deluged with phone calls. So finally, Henry stands up, clutches his heart, and falls down to the floor. George suddenly notices that something is different, goes over to Henry and says, 'Are you all right?' Henry opens his eyes, looks up and says, 'I'm sorry, but this is the only way I could get your attention.'"

Rowan & Martin's Laugh-In was for millions of viewers a cure for the Monday night blues . . . an escape from reality. The program was truly innovative in the comedy/variety series genre. Not your traditional variety show, *Laugh-In* blended political satire with freewheeling comedic sketches and wacky yet endearing characters. The program paved the way for shows like *Saturday Night Live* which would come along a decade later. However, no variety show either before or after could compare to *Laugh-In*.

"*Laugh-In* started as a one-time special in 1967. It began as a series in January 1968," recalls Gary. "We had 40 million viewers a week every Monday night; that was a huge number of people back in those days. We were serious on the set even though there was all this craziness . . . thousands of jokes going on. Although I do remember that sometimes Arte

Gary Owens in his most famous pose, as the hand-cupped-over-the-ear announcer on *Rowan & Martin's Laugh-In.*

Johnson would moon the camera as his old man character, Tyrone! Doing that show was a delightful experience. It was a great group of people that suddenly became household words from that point on. Their whole lives have been changed because of it.

"Eileen Brennan was on the show during the first season. She's a great actress. She didn't like, from what I understand, being drenched with water, hit with boxing gloves, and shot through a trap door. She left, and went back to Broadway. Goldie Hawn took her place.

"Our competition was tremendous," he continues, "and yet we still beat them frequently. There was *Gunsmoke, The Lucy Show, Monday Night Football,* and if you're going to compete with something — those were the top shows. The show was unique, and it did make a lasting impression on people. It's one of the top ten shows of TV history, at least according to all the surveys that I've seen. I'm so pleased to have been a part of it."

In addition to hosts Dan Rowan and Dick Martin, Gary Owens and Ruth Buzzi were the only two regulars to be featured in every episode of *Laugh-In.* Owens has many anecdotes from the six years he spent on the hit series.

"I remember on the first or second show we did, I came on screen and said, 'The program you are about to see is true.' They had type running across the screen that said, 'False, False, False.' And then we had a line of type which ran across the bottom of the screen continuously. It read, 'Help, I'm trapped in the newsroom! Get me out!' Well, millions of people phoned NBC saying, 'Get that poor man out of the newsroom, he's trapped!' They really thought there was some lone guy trapped in there," laughs Gary. "From that point on, no one could ever do those kinds of runners, not on our show or any comedy show! We set television back a little ways there. The network said, 'The public doesn't know the difference. You can't run those lines of type!' Isn't that strange?"

Owens was also the last person to go through the infamous trap door at the end of the first season of *Laugh-In.*

"Everybody else had experienced the trap door by the end of the first season, so I was the last one to go through. It was built for someone the size of Sammy Davis, Jr., not for a large person. I'm about six feet tall and weigh about 175 pounds," he explains. "The structure of me is different from that of Sammy Davis, Jr. When you fall down a trap door, it's like being hung suddenly, except there's not a rope around you. Even though many times there was nothing written on the script I always held, I had to look like I was reading from a script. So I had to stand there with my arms extended, which automatically makes it bad to stand over a trap door because you could break your arms.

"The first thing they did was drench me with water. The water started dripping down my glasses, and I couldn't see where I was standing. And if you can't see where you're standing, it's like touching a land mine. Suddenly, they drop me down the trap door. I hit my elbow on the way down. Fortunately, it didn't break, but it knocked a setting out of my ring. For about three weeks afterward, I'd go to NBC every night and search for the setting. I'd crawl around on the floor looking for my diamonds. Going

The 100th episode of *Laugh-In*. A cast shot with guest star John Wayne.

down a trap door looks funny, but it's not necessarily an experience you want to go through. We had many guest stars go through it including Roman Gabriel, who was a quarterback for the Rams," laughs Gary.

Another great story Owens remembers concerns legendary actor John Wayne, who was the guest star on *Laugh-In* one week.

"John Wayne was supposed to open the show impersonating me. He wore a suit exactly like mine. I had maybe three suits during all six seasons, and they would alternate those. He was supposed to wear a set of my glasses, and then put his hand over his ear. First of all, I would start out, 'From beautiful downtown Burbank.' And then there would be an explosion in front of me. John would saunter in and say, 'Fr-om beau-ti-ful down-town Bur-bank,'" says Gary, doing a perfect imitation of Wayne. "John looked up at the director and said, 'Boy, I hope I did that right.' The director said, 'That was great, Duke.' Then John Wayne said, 'I don't think I should wear the glasses.' The director said, 'Why not?' and John answered, 'Well, I'd just feel better if I didn't have to wear the glasses.' Afterwards we were talking, and he said that he felt he'd look too old with the glasses. Not that glasses indicate age. There are kids two years old who wear glasses. That was so funny!"

Gary's wonderful sense-of-the-absurd comic style lent itself perfectly to *Laugh-In*. He has also recorded no less than twenty comedy albums over the years. His MGM record "Put Your Head on My Finger" (1972) contains some of Owens' best comedy routines, including "Sure Fire Unemployment" for people who have no desire to work, and the "Lunatics Book of World Records." He also did a hilarious parody of the low-budget "School of Broadcasting" commercials called "The Golden Voice Announcers' School," in which he suggests listeners send $13,000 and a valuable heirloom to him, in care of a barbershop in Texas, in order to learn how to become a mellifluous-voiced radio announcer.

"The comedy really started as an extension of the cartoons," he theorizes. "My humor has always been a little different, because invariably I'm cast as a man who looks professional. I look like the guy who might be a bank president or the guy in the library telling you to keep quiet. But if you listen to what I say — it's pretty strange and silly! Even in high school I used to emcee a lot of things. My persona is basically a person who is an authority figure."

Owens still sees his fellow cast members from *Laugh-In* from time to time.

"I see them individually or at show business functions. I don't see Goldie Hawn or Lily Tomlin as much because they're not in town as often. I see them maybe twice a year," he says. "I see Arte Johnson, Ruth Buzzi, Jo Anne Worley and Henry Gibson quite often. I haven't seen Alan Sues in a number of years. I do the American Comedy Awards with George Schlatter every year. He's a wonderful man and a fine producer. He's been very kind to me over all these years. I loved the whole cast of *Laugh-In*. I got along with everybody."

In 1969, Gary hosted a daytime comedy show called *Letters to Laugh-In*.

"That show only ran one season," he remembers. "But it was on at 1:30

in the afternoon, which is not a good time to do a comedy show. You're on against soap operas. We'd have guests like Eartha Kitt, Mickey Rooney, Lily Tomlin and Goldie Hawn. We'd have two *Laugh-In* people and two guest stars. They would read jokes sent in by people from across the country. We received about 20,000 jokes a week. It was really a joke show. I was the emcee for it. I'll never forget when Zsa Zsa Gabor guested on the show. I announced, 'Ladies and Gentlemen—Zsa Zsa Gabor.' Well she came in, got her heel caught in the rug, and fell flat on her face! The studio audience applauded while we were all trying to get her heel loose from the rug. That was more than twenty years ago. She was always the love/hate relationship with people, even then."

In recent years, Gary has hosted the popular "Dinosaur" videos, which have won more than twenty national and international awards. He is also heard daily as the voice for ABC television promoting the network's comedy series.

In addition, Owens works with dozens of charity-related causes. He serves on the Miracle Committee for the Juvenile Diabetes Foundation. He has helped raise more than $20 million in the fight against diabetes. Owens himself was diagnosed with diabetes when he was just ten years old.

Gary has been happily married for many years to his wife, Arlette (pronounced Arleta).

"Basically, my wife and I knew each other for one week. I proposed, and we've been married ever since," he says with tenderness. "She's an interior decorator, and she majored in psychology. She's a wonderful wife and a wonderful mother for our children. She keeps very busy. I think that's the key to a happy marriage—both parties have to keep their minds very busy. There's nothing worse than one person just having to sit around all day waiting for the other one."

Gary's two sons, Scott and Chris, have followed their father into the entertainment industry, both behind the scenes and in front of the camera. Scott Owens is a TV producer who produces *America's Most Wanted,* and younger son Chris is an actor. "They grew up around show business, and they were fascinated by it. I never pushed them into it, because it is a terrible business to be pushed into," admits Gary.

Owens also owns his own production company, the Gary Owens Company, which involves all aspects of the entertainment field from television shows to sports shows to videos.

"I've always been involved in business. If you don't, it gets to be crazy. Most show business people think about business last. But you have to think about it first, because it is essentially an up and down business," explains Gary. "I've always done a lot of things every day. The only time I can work is when I've got a lot of things that I'm doing. I love it that way, it just spurs my mind."

Gary has managed to combine a strong business sense with his artistic side to become one of the more successful people in the entertainment industry.

"Everything in my life is really something I've been happy with" he says. "I never set out to make a lot of money. That was never my goal. Thank God that has happened, but my objective was never to do that. My goal was just to do creative projects and have fun with them."

Thanks to Gary Owens, we've had fun, too.

Paul Petersen

Series: *The Donna Reed Show*
Role: Jeff Stone (1958–1966)

Paul Petersen, the former child actor who portrayed Jeff Stone, Donna Reed's son on *The Donna Reed Show,* views fame as a lifetime sentence, not a career. He is a caring, intense and driven man with strong mid-America values, who is completely devoted to helping other former child actors deal with the loss of fame, and the lasting effects that child stardom has in their lives today. Petersen will get on the phone, or go and see whoever needs help, and do his best to see them through their difficulties. Although he has bitter feelings about the "business" of being a child actor, this in no way extends to his feelings about former co-stars Donna Reed, Carl Betz and Shelley Fabares. He loved Betz and Reed, and continues a close friendship with Fabares.

Charismatic and handsome, with expressive brown eyes whose warm glow of kindness can flash into fire when something strikes him as unfair, Petersen takes the problems of others — not just child actors, but the "little guy" and entertainment industry union members — personally, as if they were his own. Refreshingly candid, even outspoken, Paul is not a man who chooses his words carefully; instead, the words stream out of him from deep in his heart.

Talk show host and comedienne Joan Rivers dubbed Paul Petersen "the godfather of child actors." Why does he dedicate so much of his time to help other former child stars, and why do they choose to come to him?

"I do it because I feel compelled," states Paul. "Kid actors come to me because I've been there. Mickey Rooney and Jackie Cooper helped me after *The Donna Reed Show* went off the air, and many others in the history of Hollywood have been in my position. The bigger the star you were as a kid, the bigger the problems will be. It's just like AA, CA or anything else where a young person is undergoing a kind of trauma they can't share with quote-unquote 'civilians.' They look at me and say, 'Wait a second. Look at him. He must know.' And, of course I understand the kind of awful pain and hole that's left when ambition is driven out of you—when your influence shrinks as you go through adulthood rather than expands. The confusion of what it means with your parents. Are they responsible? Are you responsible?

"I like to tell people who are into nostalgia that we are not just some objects flickering on the screen. We're real people. All of us live in mortal fear that at even seventy-five or eighty we will just be known for what we did as children," continues Paul. "I don't want my tombstone to read 'Best known as the kid actor on *The Donna Reed Show.*' That just infuriates me. I've published fourteen books, raised children, been a businessman for twelve years—is that really the most I did in my life? I don't think so."

There have been many horror stories of stage mothers pushing their children into show business careers. Was Petersen forced into the limelight by a stage mother?

"Well, I explain to people the Darryl Hickman line, when he asked his mother why he started in show business at the age of three. She said, 'Why darling, it's because you wanted to.' Now my mother will quote exactly that. And we disagree mightily, believe me, to the point of tears," says Petersen, who believes no child is capable of making a decision with such long-lasting repercussions as becoming a professional actor. "There were awful struggles between us. Mom was a lot bigger than me. And she insisted that I take tap, ballet, singing and drums. The only point to doing all of that is to make it pay off. We lived in Los Angeles, and I was a reasonably cute kid who went on open auditions and got more than my share of work. The jobs got better and better. I gained a reputation in town, and that's wonderful except one of the jobs I went up for lasted eight years. It's as if childhood just went . . . poof. When my parents said yes to *The Donna Reed Show*, they didn't know it would last that long—but it did. I didn't understand the consequences of that work, nor did my family. I must tell you truthfully that if my family had known the consequences they would have never allowed me to do it. You know something? They didn't pay me enough. None of us gets paid enough to lose our childhood. No grown kid actor, with the exception of one, has ever put his or her kid in show business. There's a reason. We know better. If it was all so grand, where are all of our kids?"

One of Paul's pre–*Donna Reed Show* jobs was as a Mouseketeer on *The Mickey Mouse Club.* When a casting agent insisted on calling Paul "Mouse," the pugnacious nine-year-old punched him in the stomach. Paul was fired that afternoon. It would seem as though Petersen was rebelling against being in a professional environment even at that early age. This display of fiery temper did not keep him from getting other jobs, however, including *The Donna Reed Show* at the age of twelve.

After *The Donna Reed Show* went off the air, Petersen's acting career gradually went into a decline, and he tried to sedate the pain of losing

Paul Petersen

all the attention he'd once had with drugs and alcohol ("I lived the sixties, I just don't remember them," he says). Every year, Paul worked only half as much as the year before, and eventually found himself unemployable. He says casting agents his own age resented him—one later even admitted it—and forced him "to audition for parts I'd been playing all my life."

After years of complaining about what had happened to him, he decided to do something about it. This process began when he wrote his

1973 book *Walt, Mickey and Me* and has now reached the point where he can help others who are in the same boat as he once was.

"I ask myself a question when I consider new things like technology, social movements, etc. I ask myself, 'Is it safe for the children?' And I was forced to come to this question having done all the interviews for my book. I began to see this commonality with all of our (the actors') experiences. And it's true that we were all different, had different kinds of parents or grandparents or aunts or uncles. I suddenly felt the need to go outside the Mouseketeer experience. I found myself interviewing stars from a long time ago like Helen Hayes and Lillian Gish. I began to see that we all had something in common. Fame was the essential ingredient, but beyond that we had parents that thought so little of us that they traded our childhood for notoriety."

Petersen says he understands why people push their kids into show business, even though he feels it is completely wrong to do so. "I try to be charitable to parents, and not just because my mom is still alive. I think parents are impatient. When a parent looks at his or her child—and boy, do I know this," he continues with tenderness in his voice, "because my kids are all special, they're all beautiful and I want to share them with the world. But do you know when I want to share them? When they're twenty-three and twenty-four years old and can claim responsibility for what they're doing. Then I will have done my job. But the notion that I think they're so special that I'll drag them out into a professional environment at eight years old is sickening. It turns my stomach."

Did Petersen enjoy the attention while *The Donna Reed Show* was on the air?

"Sure, I loved it! It was different for me than it was for Jay North (of *Dennis the Menace* fame) who was beaten, abused and scarred deeply. I was working with wonderful people who proved their character by staying friends even after the show was over. We used to get together every month. We were the most astonishing foursome when we got together for lunch," says Paul, his tone of voice lightening. "Sometimes we were a fivesome because my little sister came along." (Petersen is referring to his sister Patty, who played Trisha Stone on *The Donna Reed Show* from 1963, when Shelley Fabares left, until 1966, when the show ended.) "Carl and I would come first because we liked to have a few drinks together. So, here you had Paul Petersen and 'Dr. Stone,' or 'Judd, for the Defense'—mind you, Carl was in that role at the time. He even won an Emmy for that series," adds Paul with pride. "And then in would walk Shelley. And then in would walk Donna Reed. People couldn't believe it. Forget that they might not recognize one of us individually, but put the four of us together, and they knew who we were. We would freak people out. We loved each other like crazy, and we were honest-to-God best pals. You have to understand how remarkable it was for a man and woman (Carl Betz and Donna Reed) in their mid–thirties to look at two youngsters like Shelley and myself, and say, 'We're going to stay close to them, no matter what, until we die.' These two talented, achieving adults reached back and *never* let us down. Now, it's true that Shelley and Donna had a very close relationship, and it was special. And Carl and I had a very special relationship. But still, we were all a family. They were so critical to my survival and Shelley's too. I miss Carl like crazy. He was the best friend I ever had." Carl Betz died in 1978, Donna Reed in 1986.

"I can't tell you how crucial Carl and Donna's friendship was to me, and Shelley's friendship remains to this day. I'll tell you how close I am to Shelley: My kids call her 'Aunt Shelley.' She loves to tease me about the fact that I was born with what she calls a vicious memory," says Paul with a smile. "I honest-to-God remember almost everything as if it happened yesterday. What I will always remember is just how much I cared about Carl and Donna. These were great people. I will always brag about them."

Does Paul ever watch reruns of *The Donna Reed Show,* and if he had to do it all over again, would he?

"Sure, I watched last night," he answers enthusiastically. "I've discovered that I'm proud of the days I spent on the show. And nobody else did it but me. I am responsible. And part of the fun is taking credit for it. I can call my pals and say 'Did you see the show last night?' Or they call me when they see an episode they especially like. It's wonderful for me.

"If I had to do it over again, I would do *The Donna Reed Show.* What I would not have done is record the records ("My Dad" and "She Can't Find Her Keys" were hits for Petersen), and go out every weekend and every hiatus to do personal appearances. I worked every single day, seven days a week, from the time I was fourteen until I was twenty-two. Why did I do all these things? It wasn't just my ego driving me. The money I made on *The Donna Reed Show* was virtually gone just keeping up a certain lifestyle. I had to work on weekends to make extra money."

Today, Paul does contract technical writing, writes articles for car magazines, sells replica sports cars and works for the cable station Nickelodeon doing personal appearances on weekends. "I love doing it, and I get to go across the country and meet all these generations of people who are still partial to shows like *The Donna Reed Show,*" he says.

Petersen also works for the Donna Reed Foundation, which provides scholarships to young people from the Midwest, where Donna Reed (née Mullenger) was born and raised, who wish to pursue a career in the performing arts *after* graduation in the university system. "There's an entire network of people who committed to Donna and her aspirations," explains Paul. "These kids can come out to Hollywood and know that they have a

A 1963 cast shot from *The Donna Reed Show*. Left to right: Shelley Fabares, Donna Reed, Carl Betz, Patty Petersen and Paul Petersen.

family out here. They won't have to worry about a place to eat or sleep. They'll know where the best managers and agents are. We're in our fifth year now. We have twelve youngsters in the university system. We're proud of them—they're good, really good. The satisfaction will be when someone notices a great actor or actress and mentions that they got their start with the Donna Reed Foundation. It's particularly appealing to me because my whole family is from Iowa, which is where we hold the Donna Reed

Festival every year. This environment (Iowa) is still where I'm most comfortable, and I still, rightly or wrongly, believe is the essence of this country. It's a little town with people who still know about things like good manners and generosity."

Still, the driving force in Petersen's life is helping out other former child actors, and trying to get laws changed in order to do this on a larger scale. The recent catalyst in Paul's life, which drove him to do everything he possibly could for "those who have served," was the suicide of Rusty Hamer, who played Rusty on *Make Room for Daddy*.

"After Rusty Hamer's death, I decided that I wasn't going to stand by and watch this anymore," says Paul. "He was exactly the same age as me, and a friend of mine. There are certain things I can't do, and one of them is keeping my mouth shut. I couldn't live with myself if I kept quiet about my feelings.

"When I went to the Screen Actors Guild, guess what I found? I didn't find what I used to find—the reluctance to admit that there was a problem. They said they'd help, and they have been helping. Being able to call up Ron Howard's office on location, and the phone rings twenty minutes later and he says, 'Who is it and how can I help?' It's going to become an industry-wide base. It's unavoidably true that there's a consequence to fame when young. The industry is beginning to recognize its responsibility. IBM, Exxon and Lockheed Aircraft are not in the business of charitable contributions. But they don't hire children like the entertainment industry does. That's the difference. All I'm asking for back is something for those unfortunates, and there are plenty. Not just young people, but adults too. I swear before I'm done, I'm going to get the laws changed. That's my mission.

"When you give up your childhood to perform you don't belong to your parents. You're not personally responsible for your life. You belong to everybody. The kids performing on shows right now are my kids. They belong to me. They belong to you, they are our kids. Other kid actors' problems are personal to me.

"The people out there on the other side of the screen are no problem at all. They want us to do well," he continues. "They have an emotional investment in us. I tell people to continue to remember not to gloat when you hear that Todd Bridges is in trouble, or Anissa Jones is dead. Damn it, these kids belong to you. They are part of your life. You don't make yourself any taller by standing on corpses."

What kinds of laws would Petersen change to benefit child actors?

"I can't figure out how come a kid actor, who already had 40 percent of his income taken from him mandatorily, can't, through the Screen Actors Guild, have a corporation set up for him," declares Paul. "I also want to know why the federal government is so desperate for money that it's got to take full tax burden from a twelve-year-old? When you're an adult you can set aside 20 percent of your income for IRA plans. Why can't we do it for kids? It makes no sense. This shows a fundamental lack of concern for our children in society. And that's got to change.

"I also think there should be ninety-day intervention where a psychologist comes and pays attention — not just for the kid but for his family. The problem is with Mom and Dad. They're the ones who cause this. Kids don't drive themselves to interviews and get their own pictures — they don't do stuff like that. Mom and Dad is the problem. The parent who puts his child in show business is telling you a lot about his character. And that character is ill-equipped to deal with the consequences of fame.

"I'll undoubtedly try to run for office in the Guild someday to try to make some sort of difference. I'm old enough and free enough to do something about these things. I'm not tilting at windmills, I am not a lonely voice in the wind. The world is changing."

We ended our interview by talking about some of Paul's professional aspirations.

"I was raised by Donna and the production staff of *The Donna Reed Show* to direct, and write and I'm good at it," he says. "Understand, that the most comfortable place I know on the planet Earth is either behind my typewriter, where I'm completely at home, or on a soundstage. After all those years of work, I know what's going on. A director is what both Donna and Carl wanted me to be. Ron Howard is like a beacon to me. People are amazed that Ron has these technical skills. Well, how the hell could he not? He grew up on soundstages and went to school afterwards. Well, of course, I don't think that will be my lasting contribution to this life."

Perhaps directing won't be his lasting contribution. Paul Petersen's enduring legacy may be even greater, and has already begun with the Petersen Commission from the Screen Actors Guild. The commission protects not only child actors on long-running television series and in films, but those who do even one popular commercial. Child actors will be grateful for years to come to this man who cared enough to turn his own unfortunate experience into something that's really making a difference in their lives.

Kasey Rogers

Series: *Peyton Place*
Role: Julie Anderson (1964–1966)
Series: *Bewitched*
Role: Louise Tate (1966–1972)

She had roles in two of the classic television series of the sixties — on opposite ends of the spectrum: first the nighttime soap opera *Peyton Place,* and then the fantasy situation comedy *Bewitched.* She has acted and written. She has raced motorcycles, and she has taught acting at her own studio. Kasey Rogers is the sort of person who is not content to watch from the sidelines, but prefers to get right in there and participate in whatever interests her.

This lovely, red-haired actress with vibrant brown eyes is vivacious, friendly and has a charming sense of humor.

Originally from the "boot heel" of Missouri, Rogers moved to Los Angeles when she was just two years old and has lived there ever since.

"My parents both come from the Midwest, from a farming background. My father was a tax consultant and my mother was a homemaker. My grandfather, my father's father, was in show business," explains Kasey regarding her family background. "I have pictures taken of my grandfather years ago from a show. He's wearing tights, and a funny little hat. He always said he would *never* allow his children to go into show business. He had ten children, and they all went into farming."

His talented granddaughter, however, forged ahead, did the forbidden, and became an actress.

"I started under contract to Paramount when I was about twenty years old. I had studied music since I was seven or eight years old . . . piano and accordion. I did little plays. I was always involved in the arts from the time I was very young," reflects Kasey. "And even when I signed with Paramount, I had some training behind me — things like the lead in the high school play. I'd also studied with a professional coach for two or three months before my contract with Paramount.

"When I signed with Paramount, they put me in a lead in a picture

113

the next week. I was not very good," she laughs in retrospect. "I wasn't really that bad either. I was very proper. I'd stand very straight and mind my 'Ps' and 'Qs' and all that while I was supposed to be acting naturally. I was in a number of classics but in small roles."

Rogers, who acted under the stage name Laura Elliot while at Paramount, had small roles in *Sampson and Delilah* and *The Great Gatsby* (1949) with Alan Ladd and *A Place in the Sun* (1951).

As Laura Elliot, Kasey also had a couple of lead roles in westerns like *The Denver and the Rio Grande* (1952), where she played opposite Edmund O'Brien, Sterling Hayden and ZaSu Pitts. "She was wonderful," says Kasey about ZaSu. "She and I were the only two women. I was also in *Silver City* (1951) with Edmund O'Brien and Yvonne DeCarlo. I played the bad girl," she adds with delight. "I was lucky to do a number of fun pictures and also very good pictures at Paramount."

It was on loan-out to Warner Brothers that Kasey made her favorite film, Alfred Hitchcock's *Strangers on a Train* (1951). In the classic suspense film, Rogers brilliantly portrayed Miriam Joyce Haines, a most unlikeable character. In the film, Kasey's ravishing good looks were downplayed with thick cat glasses. "I remember when we were on tour promoting the film nobody recognized me because of the glasses," she says.

Rogers' unforgettable scene in *Strangers on a Train*, where Miriam is strangled in an amusement park, has to be one of film's all-time great murder scenes. The terror in Rogers' eyes is chilling.

"I loved doing that film because I played such a bitch," she laughs. "I love roles like Miriam because they really are a lot more fun. You get to be so bitchy, and show all the sides of yourself that you don't show to the world. There's a little bit of you in every character that you do. It's a little slice of your personality which you pull out and expand upon.

"The more difficult roles are like Robert Morse, who is doing the play *Tru*, which is a wonderful, complete sublimation of his own characteristics and traits to this other person—Truman Capote," she elaborates. "And he is incredible. Robert DeNiro, Meryl Streep and a few others really lose as much of themselves as possible. But basically, Bette Davis is still Bette Davis. I don't care if she's Queen Elizabeth or Apple Annie—she's still Bette Davis."

Following her contract at Paramount, Rogers acted in hundreds of television shows including *The Lucy Show, Perry Mason, 77 Sunset Strip, Maverick, Hawaii Five-O* and *The Thin Man.*

Her first regular series role was as Julie Anderson, the mother of Betty (played by Barbara Parkins) in the huge hit prime-time soap opera *Peyton Place.* In today's soap operas children grow from being a tot to a teenager in record time—a few months or a year—which leaves eighteen- or nineteen-year-old characters with thirty-year-old parents. This amusing

Kasey Rogers

and disconcerting soap opera trait must have begun with *Peyton Place*, because there's no way Rogers could have actually been Parkins' mother.

"*Peyton Place* was the first big nighttime show, and it paved the way for *Dynasty* and *Dallas*. The most highly recognizable I was, was when *Peyton Place* hit the air. I had done hundreds of television shows and pictures before that," points out Kasey. "I can remember one day Barbara Parkins and I went shopping in Beverly Hills. It was after work and before *Peyton Place* had actually aired. The next time we went shopping was the day after the first *Peyton Place* had aired. We were mobbed, we couldn't go anywhere. People were screaming, 'Peyton Place! Peyton Place!'

"And then when I was on *Bewitched*, they had me wear a black wig because the first actress who played Louise had black hair. I was on *Bewitched* four or five years and people would still say, 'You're Julie Anderson from *Peyton Place*.' And I'd say, 'Do you ever watch *Bewitched*?' And

Kasey Rogers and Farley Granger in Alfred Hitchcock's *Strangers on a Train* (1951).

they'd say, 'Yes.' And I'd ask, 'Do you know the boss's wife, Louise Tate?' And they'd say, 'Yes.' And then they'd know me. The black wig threw them off. I had a degree of anonymity, and yet a certain recognizability. It was the perfect balance.

"Recently, I was in a fast food restaurant, trying to pick something up in a hurry. The line took forever. This man said to me, 'Weren't you on *Bewitched?*' And I said that I was. Then everyone started to say, 'I knew it!' People don't usually say anything. They think they know me but they're not sure. I love it. I don't think I would like to be mobbed every place I'd go."

Rogers took over the role of Louise Tate from actress Irene Vernon almost immediately after leaving *Peyton Place.*

"*Bewitched* and *Peyton Place* started the same year. I was on *Peyton Place* for two years. I know it was 252 episodes because I still have the scripts," says Kasey. "I had always adored watching *Bewitched* while I was on *Peyton Place.* I said to myself, 'Oh, my God! I get to be on *Bewitched!*' I was thrilled. I thought *Bewitched* was the cutest show. I just loved it. I left *Peyton Place* when it went to color, and started *Bewitched* when it went to color. So all of my *Bewitched* episodes are in color.

"It was a very interesting transition," says Kasey about going from a nighttime soap to a fantasy sitcom. "I had done comedy before, but after 252 episodes of *Peyton Place*, where everything is internalized and so dramatic—and then I went to *Bewitched*, where everything was light. I was still internalizing. And they'd say, 'Come on and loosen up, Kasey!'. Then I'd switch to the comedy mode and every thing was fine.

"It was a difficult transition only because I had not done comedy in so long. I remember the first script I received when I was on *Bewitched*. Here I adored this series, and when I got the script I said to myself, 'This isn't very funny. I guess this isn't one of their better scripts.' And then we had a read-through with Elizabeth Montgomery and Dick York, and everything started happening. It was very funny. You have to really look for the humor, find it and then make it funny.

"And now, when I teach my students, I definitely show the kids the difference between comedy and drama ... the truth in each of them and the techniques you need."

On *Bewitched*, Samantha and Darrin were an extremely lovey-dovey couple when some kind of magic wasn't going on to upset things. Larry and Louise Tate represented more of the typical married couple. They argued about things that most married couples argue about.

In one episode, Louise decides to leave Larry because he didn't choose her to be on his volleyball team. When he finally comes to pick her up at the Stevens' house, she asks, "Why didn't you pick me for the team?" Larry replies, "Because I wanted to win." A remark any husband might make.

Larry Tate, played to perfection by David White, was the ultimate yes man. He'd agree with anything to get an account for his advertising agency. In real life, most of us have worked with someone like Larry. His chic wife Louise was the only one who could really set him straight. She always kept her composure, always said and did the right thing, except when witchcraft was at work, causing her to momentarily doubt her sanity. When I mentioned to Kasey that I thought Louise was a very tolerant wife to put up with Larry, Kasey laughed and said, "Either very tolerant or very stupid!"

In the episode "Mixed Doubles," Louise and Samantha trade places because of some magical molecular disturbance. Louise wakes up with Darrin, and Samantha with Larry. This was kind of kinky for *Bewitched*—sort of a *Bob and Carol and Ted and Alice* in sitcom form. By this time, they had let Kasey take off the black wig and allowed her to play the role with her own natural auburn hair.

The character of Louise was almost always sensible and level-headed, except when arguing with her husband. Even when she'd sometimes witness the same magical insanity as the Stevens' screaming neighbor,

Rogers with TV husband David White in a scene from *Bewitched*.

Gladys Kravitz, Louise would still keep her cool and even offer sympathy for the hysterical Mrs. Kravitz by muttering, "That poor woman."

One of Rogers' funniest scenes on *Bewitched* (from a script written by Robert Riley Crutcher) took place at one of the client dinner parties. Larry is extolling the virtues of his mother-in-law (a woman he really can't stand) for the benefit of a client, while Kasey as Louise does a marvelous slow burn. Finally, not able to take it anymore, she gives her husband a swift, hard kick under the dining room table and escorts him out of the room, saying, "Excuse me, dear, I was just crossing my legs. Let's go into the living room where the light is better. I want to make sure I haven't broken the skin." Larry, hobbling away, says, "It's a wonder you didn't break my leg."

Another great line that Kasey as Louise often delivered was: "You know something, Larry? You're sick!"

Rogers remembers the late David White and the cast of *Bewitched* with great fondness.

"David White was superb. His looks, his reactions—he really knew his comedy. And he knew exactly what he was doing in that role. I just thought he was great. Everyone in the cast was wonderful. Elizabeth

Montgomery, Dick York . . . everyone. Agnes Moorehead (Endora) was fantastic. Even off the screen she'd say, 'I love the illusion of it all!'" says Kasey, doing a marvelous impression of the actress with her arms raised in a theatrical gesture. "That was Agnes, on or off screen. People really play themselves most of the time. I don't think Paul Lynde (Uncle Arthur) could play anything but Paul Lynde. Try to think of him in a serious role and you can't!" she laughs. "I loved him in everything he did."

Regarding Marion Lorne, who endearingly played the sweet, bumbling witch Aunt Clara, Kasey says: "Interestingly enough, Marion Lorne's first picture in the United States was *Strangers on a Train*. Alfred Hitchcock brought her over from England to do the role. I was privileged to be in her first picture here and her last series. She was just adorable. Off screen she was just like she was on screen. In later years, when she was reaching for words," laughs Kasey, "she was really reaching for words! Marion had darling mannerisms, and she made them work for her."

When asked for an anecdote from *Bewitched*, Rogers hesitates and then replies: "One thing just popped into my mind out of the blue. It was late one afternoon and we were shooting a scene. It was one of the dinner parties at Samantha's home. The table looked beautiful. And there were wine glasses. The director said, 'Roll 'em, shoot, take!' And it was real wine," she laughs. "Well, we never had real wine. Elizabeth had poured real wine into the glasses. And then when the director shouted, 'Who put the wine in the glasses?' Elizabeth just sat there with this cute, devilish smile on her face."

Rogers hasn't really stayed in close touch with her former co-stars. "The only one I've really stayed in touch with is Sandra Gould (Gladys Kravitz). Sandy and I knew each other before. We did a play together years and years before *Bewitched*. We have kept in contact on and off over the years. Usually if you call someone, it's about business matters. Yet any one of the people I've worked with I could call, like Mia Farrow or Barbara Parkins, and say 'How are you doing?' We always pick up where we left off when we do talk. There's something that lasts. You don't forget each other."

In real life, Rogers has been married twice and has four children and two grandchildren. "They've all grown and flown," she says. Her children have all gone into artistic lines of work. Her eldest son, James Donnellan, received a Grammy nomination for sound engineering. Both of her daughters, Mona and Monika Lewis, studied acting. Mona eventually became an artist, and Monika is involved in video productions. Her youngest son, Michael Lewis, once raced motorcycles, and is now an audio consultant.

It was through her youngest son that Rogers became a motorcycle racer herself. She was nicknamed "Kasey" 'because she could out-hit any boy in baseball while in grammar school. Obviously, some of that tomboy spirit has stayed with her. Rogers put on the Women's Nationals for four years and raced all over the country from the time *Bewitched* ended in 1972 until 1979. She also wrote a motorcycle column for a leading Los Angeles newspaper where a picture of Kasey wearing a helmet appeared weekly. "I became a photo journalist and took all of my own action photos. I've also written a couple of screenplays. One was produced as an episode of *Wagon Train*," says the versatile Rogers.

One of the things she finds most rewarding these days is not only acting herself but teaching acting. Students used to come to her home in Southern California from as far away as Arizona. It was getting crowded, so she decided to expand and open her own studio in North Hollywood, California, which she calls the Hollywood Underground Network. Now the actress plans to open more Hollywood Underground Network acting studios across the country.

"Teaching is a real high for me. When everyone's adrenaline is flowing, it challenges me as a teacher tremendously," she says enthusiastically. "Every student is so different. They have different talents, varied goals and hang-ups. As a teacher, I have to zero in and clarify things. What works for one student won't work for another.

"Studying acting can change a person's life. I've had bratty, obnoxious teenagers on drugs. And they'd get off drugs, their appearance changes, they start developing self-esteem and become really nice, good people. For some, even if they don't go on to become actors, just seeing themselves on camera and learning changes their lives," continues the actress, who uses a video camera when teaching. "Recently, in a few months, I watched one young man change from a cute, roly-poly character actor into a young leading man. He started working out and lost twenty pounds. Now I have an extended family which are my students. I really seem to get involved with their lives to (I try and make it) a limited extent. But sometimes you do become involved because there are some people you think are wonderful . . . they train and study so hard. You find that they're deserving of breaks. I make my classes like an actual set so they'll feel at home when they do start working on a soundstage.

"I've started some casting director workshops, and I've had some of the very finest casting directors, some of the top people in town, come and do workshops with the kids. And many have called, and my students have worked because of the workshop.

"Those students who make it have to have this dedication. They love acting, the entire career, ambience . . . everything about it. Unless it's really in your heart to be an actor—then don't do it. If it is in your heart, no one can stop you."

Spoken well by one who knows. You can be sure that nothing ever stops Kasey Rogers.

Rose Marie

Series: *The Bob Cummings Show*
Recurring role (1955–1959)
Series: *My Sister Eileen*
Role: Bertha (1960–1961)
Series: *The Dick Van Dyke Show*
Role: Sally Rogers (1961–1966)
Series: *The Doris Day Show*
Role: Myrna Gibbons (1969–1971)

From the time Rose Marie was a toddler, show business has been an immense part of her life. As Baby Rose Marie, she was one of the most famous children in the country. Later on, she would become a household name again as the wisecracking comedy writer Sally Rogers on *The Dick Van Dyke Show*.

It all began for the New York-born Rose Marie Mazzetta at a tender time in life. Rose Marie's parents were not in show business, but her mother used to take her to the theater quite often.

"I won an amateur contest when I was three years old," remembers Rose. "My mother used to take me to all the shows and everything. I would come back singing, dancing and imitating everyone I saw. My mother's neighbors entered me in the amateur contest. My mother was petrified, because she didn't know if I would perform or not in front of an audience. Our neighbors bought my dress and my shoes, and I sang "What Can I Say Dear After I Say I'm Sorry?" I brought the house down, and I won . . . I think it was twenty bucks. My family then took me to Atlantic City. I was singing on the beach with some kids. Someone from a radio station in Atlantic City on the Steel Pier heard me, and asked my father if I could go on the air. I had a show that I sang on from the Steel Pier."

Rose Marie has an incredibly sharp memory, and actually recalls winning that contest when she was just three years old.

"I remember winning the contest but I don't actually remember singing. In fact, that relates to the title of the book I'm supposed to be writing,"

Rose Marie

she says with a smile. "When I came off the stage at the contest, the audience was yelling and screaming. Just imagine a three-year-old child singing like a grown-up.

"I never sounded like a child—that was the amazing part of it. I sounded then as I do now," explains the husky-voiced entertainer. "I came off the stage and someone put a bouquet of red roses in one hand, and another bouquet in the other hand. I had them in both of my hands, and I said, 'Hold the roses, I can't take my bow.' I went out and took a bow because they were all yelling and screaming. I dropped the roses and went out there.

"'Hold the Roses, I Can't Take My Bow' is the title of my book. I've worked very spasmodically on it. I did a presentation for a publisher, and they flipped over it. They wanted two chapters, and I said, 'When I have time,' she adds with a laugh.

From the radio show in Atlantic City, Baby Rose Marie went on to star in her own national show on radio, where she sang the same popular songs that adults were doing.

"When I was five years old I had my own coast-to-coast radio program on NBC on Sunday mornings at 12:15," she recalls. "There was an announcer, a piano player, and myself. The sponsor was Julius Grossman Shoes, which is still there, by the way. The funny part is that although my program was on coast-to-coast, Julius Grossman Shoes only had one store, in New York. I think that's really very funny! I was signed to NBC along with Amos and Andy, Rudy Vallee and Vincent Lopez. People used to write in to NBC and say, 'That's not a child, it's a forty-five-year-old midget. No child sings like that.' NBC was affiliated with RKO, so I did personal appearances for fifty-two weeks one year in theaters across the country, just to prove that I was indeed a child."

Following her childhood stardom, one of Rose Marie's first big hits was *Top Banana* on stage with Phil Silvers in 1951. Did she enjoy doing the show?

"Very much so. I mean a hit Broadway show is always nice to have on your resume," she answers with that same famous tongue-in-cheek delivery which made her famous yet again as Sally Rogers on *The Dick Van Dyke Show*.

Before she received the role on *The Dick Van Dyke Show*, Rose had a recurring role on *The Bob Cummings Show* and played Bertha on the short-lived situation comedy *My Sister Eileen*. She also did "every guest shot imaginable on TV."

By the time of *The Dick Van Dyke Show*, Rose had already struck up friendships with Danny Thomas and Sheldon Leonard. She used to tease them about why she hadn't had a chance yet to do a guest-shot role on *The Danny Thomas Show*. When they called her, she thought it was to do a guest-starring role on the Thomas program, but was happily surprised to find out that they wanted her for a regular role on *The Dick Van Dyke Show*. Carl Reiner met her, and he cast Rose immediately as the female comedy writer.

Originally, *The Dick Van Dyke Show* had been written and created by Carl Reiner as a show called *Head of the Family*. Reiner himself planned to star in the series as the comedy writer that Dick Van Dyke would later portray.

"Carl Reiner had written the script and had made a pilot with himself as the star. Barbara Britton was to play his wife, Sylvia Miles played my part and Marty Brill was in Morey Amsterdam's part," remembers Rose. "In fact, we saw the pilot. Carl also showed it to Sheldon Leonard. Sheldon told Carl, 'I like the script, I like the idea, but I don't like you in it.' Carl had written thirteen scripts by this time. He went to New York and saw Dick Van Dyke in *Bye Bye Birdie*. He asked Dick, 'How would you like to do a television show?' And that's how it all came about."

The Dick Van Dyke Show was a departure from the majority of sit-coms aired during the early sixties. In other shows, they referred to a character's job but rarely showed the main character's place of work. In *The Dick Van Dyke Show,* the office scenes are among the best.

A typical office scene showed how the television writers worked. Dick Van Dyke, as head writer Rob Petrie, would be doing push-ups; Morey Amsterdam, as Buddy Sorrell, would be reclining on the couch looking as though he was ready for a nap, and Rose Marie as Sally would be filing her nails. While all this activity was going on, the writers were brainstorming ideas for the mythical *Alan Brady Show.* Anyone who has ever had the opportunity to watch TV writers at work knows that this is a realistic scene. Very rarely are they sitting at their desks behind their typewriters.

In an age where working women were shown in the stereotypical roles of secretary or school teacher, Rose Marie as Sally Rogers really portrayed television's first career woman who had a job equal to that of a man. As the female television comedy writer, she contributed just as much to the show as the men.

In the episode "The Pen Is Mightier Than the Mouth," Rob and Buddy get to see what working without Sally would be like after she becomes a smash success on a talk show and ponders leaving *The Alan Brady Show.* In this episode, Rob comments, "Working with Buddy without Sally is like playing football without a helmet."

Rose Marie's role was actually based on real-life comedy writers Selma Diamond and Lucille Kallen.

"I knew about Selma Diamond, but I never knew about the other one," admits Rose. "I knew that Carl must have fashioned my role out of somebody. But then I really played myself. I usually play myself when I do a role.

"I have been told before that I was the first liberated woman on TV," she continues. "I worked with the guys on an equal basis. Show business has never been a case of—woman and man. Nor color, religion, race or anything. Our business has always been, 'How much talent do you have?' And that's the wonderful thing about show business. Nobody ever worries about whether you're black or orange or green or blue, or whether you're Catholic or not—it boils down to 'How much talent do you have?' And I think that was the same thing that prevailed when Selma was writing for other people. I don't think they looked at her as a woman per se; I think they looked at her as a co-worker."

Before the casting on *The Dick Van Dyke Show* was completed, Rose Marie suggested her old friend Morey Amsterdam—a writer himself, known as "the human joke machine"—as the third writer in the comedy team.

"I met Morey when I was twelve years old. We worked together. We've been friends over the years, I'm his daughter's godmother," she points out with pride.

Morey Amsterdam and Rose Marie had such great chemistry together in the office scenes, it would have been great if the producers had cast them as a married couple. Of course, many of the plots on the series concerned man-hungry Sally being single. And Amsterdam's character, Buddy, had a wife named Pickles. The writers did sort of explore the possibility of a secret romance in the episode "The Secret Life of Buddy and Sally." In this episode, Rob finds out that Buddy and Sally are sneaking off together on the weekends. He assumes that they are having an affair, follows them up to a lodge, and discovers they are moonlighting as performers doing a nightclub act.

"In those days they didn't have spin-offs," explains Rose. "I think if they had done a spin-off series, they would have paired us together. A few years ago, Barbara Corday came to me with an idea for a spin-off, and so did Brandon Tartikoff. They each had different ideas. One concerned Dick (as Rob Petrie), who because of his alcoholism had lost his job. Morey and I were to be living in California, we find him, and bring him back with us and start all over again. Only this time, Morey and I were married. That was one of the ideas. The other idea was about his son Ritchie growing up to be a writer, and asking us to help him. There have been some good ideas knocked around, but nobody has ever done anything about them."

Rose Marie remembers the set of *The Dick Van Dyke Show* as an extremely happy one where actors were even encouraged to contribute ideas for scripts.

"We had a very good time. I think that comes across in our performances because we just loved it," says Rose. "Everybody contributed towards the scripts. When we would do my 'Aunt Agnes' lines, Carl would come up with a couple, Morey would come up with a couple, and our script girl, Marjorie Mullen, would write them all down in her book. She'd write them under the heading 'S.O.S.,' which stood for 'some other show.' And she'd mention things we didn't use in other shows that might be perfect for the show we were doing.

"When we'd first come in on a Wednesday morning, we used to talk for about an hour," she continues. "And everybody would kick around

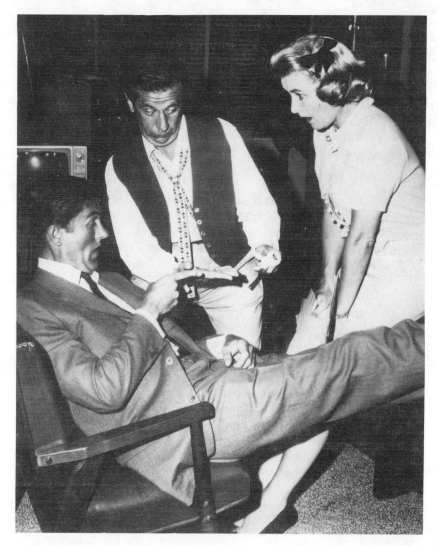

Dick Van Dyke, Morey Amsterdam and Rose Marie cutting up offstage during an episode of *The Dick Van Dyke Show.*

ideas. They'd talk about different things that happened to them. Carl incorproated a lot of the stories, and then a lot of writers came up with different ideas too."

Rose relates another story that shows how indispensable script girl Marjorie Mullen was to the program. It concerns the episode entitled "The Twizzle." In this episode, Sally premieres a new song and dance, somewhat based on "The Twist," at a bowling alley.

"There was a show where we did the Twizzle. The first scene just would not work. We were almost up to show time. We broke for dinner and went into the commissary. We said, 'Let's try and work on this thing.' We were all exchanging opinions when we finally came up with an idea. Morey said, 'That's great!' and then he said, 'But nobody wrote this down.' And Margie said, 'I have it here on a napkin. I'll go in and type this up and give it to you.' And she did. That's the scene we ended up doing, and it worked out fine."

Playing the only single female character on the show, Rose Marie had some wonderful episodes which featured Sally believing she was in love with various men. Of course, none of them were good enough for her.

Rose Marie gave a poignant performance in the episode "Jilting the Jilter," in which a selfish comedian proposes to Sally just so he can get a new act for free. When she realizes this, she handles it with a lot of class — showing good-natured bravado on the outside, but with an undercurrent of touching vulnerability.

One of the funniest and first episodes that featured Rose was "Sally Is a Girl." As you might remember, Sally was always considered one of the boys. When Rob used the term "fellas," he was talking about Sally too. In this particular episode, Rob's wife, Laura (Mary Tyler Moore), convinces her husband to stop treating Sally as one of the guys. Rob becomes overly solicitous, causing Buddy and Mel (Richard Deacon) to think the two are having an affair. Even Rob thinks Sally's in love with him. Wise woman that she was, Sally knew all along what was going on and was just flattered by the attention.

Rose Marie has many favorite episodes of *The Dick Van Dyke Show*.

"I loved the one where I'm disappointed on my birthday. I loved our Christmas show because we all got a chance to do an act on the show within a show. There are very few that I don't like," she reflects. "'Romance, Roses and Rye Bread,' where I have a secret admirer, was a very good show, and a special one for me."

One thing the actress didn't expect was for the show to go on for decades.

"No, we had no idea that would happen. If we did, I think everybody would have gotten more money. None of us are getting residuals," she confides. "I thought I had a very good deal at the time. Let's say I made $100 for a particular episode. That show would be shown six times, and I would get another $100. I thought that was a hell of a deal because it was 100 percent residuals. Some people only had 50 percent or 75 percent residuals. When the sixth show was shown, that was it — it was over. And no matter where I go, and no matter what I do, that show is on all over the country. Today when you do a show, you get a residual. I mean, I've gotten residuals for thirty-six cents. It's amazing, I get residuals from shows like *Gunsmoke,* but not the Van Dyke show. And I did *Gunsmoke* before I did the Van Dyke show."

Rose Marie had a regular role on another series during the sixties. She co-starred as secretary Myrna Gibbons on *The Doris Day Show.* One way it was similar to *The Dick Van Dyke Show* was that they would have office party scenes where Rose got the chance to showcase her talent by singing as well as doing impersonations, like her famous Jimmy Durante.

"I just adore Doris. We had a wonderful time. She's a marvelous, lovely lady. I don't feel she's given the credit for as much talent as she has," says Rose.

In recent years, Rose has appeared on the hit television series *Murphy Brown.* She also did a musical act with Rosemary Clooney, Margaret Whiting and Helen O'Connell called *4 Girls 4.* The entertainer loves to perform before a live audience.

"You have to make the audience like you, laugh with you, and enjoy. In other words, you control it. And if they like you and go with you it's sheer heaven," she says.

"That's why we did the Van Dyke show in front of an audience, because we are all basically stage performers. We loved the idea of having an audience reaction that was honest. And that has a lot to do with comedy. You need an honest reaction. When I did *The Bob Cummings Show,* they filmed it and then they ran it in a theater to get the laughs. I was with him for four or five years, and learned an awful lot from him. Bob was wonderful. He was just great."

During her lifelong career, Rose has made many friends in the entertainment industry. She still sees many of her former co-stars.

"I talk to Doris Day every once in a while. I went to see her in Carmel once. Morey, I see all the time. I see Mary Tyler Moore whenever I go to New York. Richard Deacon passed away. He was my love—a good, good friend. Before he passed away, I saw Bob Cummings on his eightieth birthday. Dick, I see once in a while. I see Larry Matthews at different openings. He's on the other side of the camera now," she ways with pride about the actor who played young Ritchie on *The Dick Van Dyke Show.*

"As far as close friends are concerned, Morey is the closest friend I have out of the show. I was also very close to Danny Thomas. I have an awful lot of friends, but not necessarily close friends in the business."

There's talk of starring Rose Marie in her own series based on a play she's toured with called *Up a Tree.* The series would be entitled *Ring Around Rosie.* In this new series, she would play a councilperson.

"I have very high hopes for the show," she says. "I think it's very much 'today,' and nothing else has been done quite like it. It makes the woman very important, and I think that's the way we are."

Rose Marie says she's done everything in show business except the circus and opera.

"I wish I would have had a chance to work with Laurence Olivier. I would have loved to have met him and worked with him. I've done stage, Broadway, television, radio and movies. I mean there isn't a hell of a lot that I haven't done. It really has all been very nice. I've had a very, very full career."

James Stacy

Series: *The Adventures of Ozzie and Harriet*
Role: Fred (1958–1964)
Series: *Lancer*
Role: Johnny Madrid Lancer (1968–1970)

A powerful actor and a man of great integrity, a man who has demonstrated more courage in hiw own life than could ever be written in a script, James Stacy tackles life's obstacles with an aggressiveness and tenacity which are a part of his strength.

Tragically maimed in a 1973 motorcycle accident, Stacy has continued creating as an artist. He acts as well as writes and produces screenplays. A person with less strength might have crumbled under the strain, but Jim has kept going. He acts in projects that show the disabled in a positive light rather than in limited, old-fashioned stereotypes. By doing this, he not only entertains but educates the public as well.

One of those men who gets better looking as he matures, Stacy has overwhelming dark good looks . . . coal black hair, a roguish twinkle in his eye and that devastating smile which has graced many a long, lingering close-up. He has a great sense of humor and smiles a lot — both in real life and on camera.

Born Maurice Elias, he grew up in Burbank, California, surrounded by studios such as Warner Bros. and NBC.

"I used to go to the movies all the time. I loved Westerns. I remember when it was a quarter to get in. As a kid, it really never occurred to me to become an actor. I wanted to be a fireman," Jim admits with a chuckle.

The first time Jim remembers acting was while he was a student at John Burroughs High School. "I remember doing things in the auditorium in front of an audience like pantomiming to the song 'White Cliffs of Dover,'" reminisces Stacy. "I also read for the senior play, which was *Harvey* that year. I was so nervous. I remember thinking, 'How do actors get rid of this nervousness?'"

As you walk into Stacy's home, you notice a large, framed print of James Dean hanging on the wall. When I asked if he liked James Dean,

131

Jim answered that he did, and mentioined that he even met him once when he was a teenager.

"I was at Bob's Big Boy in Burbank. I saw this Porsche parked out in the lot and went out to look at it. I talked to this old guy for a while about the car. I told him my name and asked what his was. He said, 'James Dean.' I said, 'You're kind of old to be James Dean, aren't you?' He was in make-up for *Giant*—they had him made up to look about forty years older than he was. I didn't recognize him," laughs Stacy.

A couple of his friends, the late Richard Boone of the series *Have Gun Will Travel* and Bob Fuller who starred on *Laramie*, encouraged Stacy to try acting. Jim even attended Boone's acting class. While Stacy was playing football at Glendale College, a scout spotted him and signed him to play for the Vancouver, B.C., Lions.

"I played there for a month, and then I was traded to Montreal. I played there for a month and then they cut me. I was nineteen years old, had $500 on me, and went to New York and got a job doing advertising for DeVega stores. While I was working there, I decided to go to acting class again."

However, what really seemed to hook Stacy into acting was a summer that he spent working as an extra in films.

"The whole atmosphere was exciting," he remembers with a smile. "I was really pushy and very aggressive. I'd go to the director and say, 'Is there anything else I can do?' or 'Can I say that line?' 'Maybe if I ad-lib something they'll pay attention to me.' Then I'd think to myself, 'Maybe I should run over and bump into that actor.' I used to drive the directors insane. I was always pushing to do something more. They'd yell, 'For the last time, no! Now get outta here!' I did it in a sort of cute, funny way—so they liked me. Sometimes it worked!"

Following a vacation tour of Europe, Stacy returned to Hollywood, where he received his first regular series role as David and Rick Nelson's fraternity brother, Fred, on *The Adventures of Ozzie and Harriet*.

"I was so scared when I had my first speaking part on *Ozzie and Harriet*. It was nerve-wracking. I pulled myself out of it, though. I was actually giving Mr. Nelson acting lessons. I'd say, 'This is how I work. Give me a color to work with.' And he'd say, 'Color? What's this color stuff? Just read the line!' I'd tell him about the stuff I was learning in acting school," laughs Jim heartily.

Stacy became friends with both David and Rick, and seems to have great affection for the entire Nelson family. In fact, he had talked with David Nelson on the day of our interview.

"Rick and David rented this house, it was the first cliff-hanger house in Hollywood. Oh my Lord, when I think of those days," remembers Jim. "Rick and David had everything Japanese style. Everything was low on the

James Stacy

ground. You sat on the floor. It was good, clean fun in those days. No drugs. The old man (referring to Ozzie Nelson) was always worried about that. I remember once I took the tea out of a tea bag, rolled it in a piece of paper, and started smoking it. The cameraman and everyone on the set was looking at me in complete shock. Mr. Nelson and everyone started sniffing the cigarette, and saying, 'Are you sure that's just tea? What is that really?'" Jim laughs at the memory.

"I also remember Elvis and his buddies challenging us (Rick Nelson's team) to football games when they were in town from Graceland. We'd play two out of three games at the house in Bel Air. No one was there. No cameras. We'd pull up, the ten of us, in Rick's Cadillac with the top down. And Elvis would already be there. Rick would walk right up to where Elvis was standing with his hands on his hips. They'd be eyeball to eyeball, and Elvis would ask, 'You guys ready to play?' And Rick would accept the challenge. By the way, we won," remembers Jim with pride.

Stacy makes his way over to his bookcase, reaches for the top shelf, and pulls down a copy of Ozzie Nelson's 1973 autobiography, *Ozzie*.

"When I first started working for the Nelsons my name was still Maurice Elias. I hadn't changed it yet." He turns the pages of the book to an inscription, and says, "This really means a lot to me." The inscription reads:

> To Maurice alias Jim alias Fred
> Who possesses the rare qualities of integrity, talent and courage
> With Love and Admiration from Ozzie.

"Ozzie was very proud of me because after I'd done about a year of *Ozzie and Harriet*, I got a part on *The Donna Reed Show*. It was my first really good part. Well, I had a part on the Ozzie show that week. So, I went to Mr. Nelson and told him I had a part on Donna Reed. I asked, 'Can I get off this week?' And he said, 'Sure. Go ahead.' And I said, 'You won't get another Fred, will you?' He said, 'Don't worry, go ahead and do the show.'

"The part on *The Donna Reed Show* that I had," he continues, "was as Shelley Fabares' boyfriend, Johnny. In one scene, I was climbing up a ladder decorating the gym for a dance, and she was rehearsing. She sings this song to me called 'Johnny Angel.' And I remember, I was up on the ladder smiling at her. At the time, I didn't know what 'Johnny Angel' was. It became a big hit. I remember hearing it on the radio lots of times. And whenever the song came on the radio, I'd tell whoever I was with, 'Hey ... I was that guy. I'm Johnny Angel.' Of course, nobody believed me," he laughs. (This *Donna Reed Show* episode was entitled "Donna's Primadonna.")

"Ozzie Nelson was a great man. You know, other people have mentioned me in their autobiographies. But Mr. Nelson was such a sweet guy, he sent me a copy. The others didn't. I remember when he was on his deathbed, and Mrs. Nelson said he was going fast. Man, I wanted to go and see him. He was the kind of guy who would fight death ... you know ... hang on," says Jim quietly, remembering a man for whom he obviously had a great deal of respect.

Wayne Maunder and James Stacy in an episode of the western series *Lancer*.

One of Stacy's early film roles, in 1957, was in the film *Sayonara*, which starred Marlon Brando and was directed by Josh Logan. Jim played a brash *Stars and Stripes* reporter. In the interracial love story, Brando's character is going to propose to a Japanese actress, portrayed by Miko Taka. Jim's reporter character knows Brando's reasons for being in Tokyo and tries to get a story out of him. Even though it was a small part, Stacy says this role was one of his favorites.

"We were supposed to be in Tokyo. I say, 'I'm from *Stars and Stripes*. What are you doing in Tokyo, sir?' Brando says, 'I'm just passing through.' Then I ad-libbed the line, 'Just seeing the sights, huh?' Brando shot this look back at me—Wham!—I thought, 'Oh, no! He's mad at me.' I was playing a smart ass, so I just ad-libbed the line," laughs Jim. "Brando turned to Josh Logan and said, 'Let the boy keep that in.'"

The series for which Stacy is probably best known is the sixties western *Lancer*, in which he played Johnny Madrid Lancer, a drifter and gunfighter with a lightning-fast draw. He was the son of Murdoch Lancer, portrayed by Andrew Duggan. Wayne Maunder played Scott Lancer, the other son—a sophisticated college graduate from Boston. Each son was from a different marriage of Murdoch Lancer's. The sons were as different as night and day—one blonde, the other dark; one trusting, the other suspicious.

"Actually, I was supposed to do a show in Europe and Asia," says Stacy regarding the series role. "About six months later, they offered me *Lancer*. It was strange because I'd always loved Westerns. It was like I was subconsciously living out a kid's dream—riding a horse and shooting from the hip. I enjoyed it. I was fulfilling my saddle fantasies," he laughs.

Stacy's role was the more interesting of the two brothers. Johnny was a moody sort of guy. "It seems they've cast me as such a sad puss since *Lancer*," points out Jim. "On *Ozzie and Harriet*, I was funny and cute. I think if I hadn't been such a sad sack on *Lancer*—you know, so serious— that I would have done a lot more comedy."

Jim played Johnny with a quiet yet fiery intensity, as he has played many of his roles. Stacy's soft-spoken manner is perfect for the camera. His expressive eyes convey an honesty that can't be faked. Stacy's favorite *Lancer* episode is the one where Johnny is blinded.

Lancer isn't the only western Stacy has acted in. He's done quite a few television shows and films in the genre. He was featured in a couple of episodes of *Gunsmoke*, including an episode titled "Yankton." In this particular episode he plays a saddle tramp who rides into Dodge City to romance the daughter of the richest man in town (played by Forrest Tucker). Written by Jim Byrnes, the plot of "Yankton" is unpredictable and completely engrossing. Stacy does an outstanding job of not giving away anything about the title character. The audiences senses that he is holding something back, and they wonder if the character is good, bad or somewhere in between.

Stacy seems to be at his best playing brash-yet-charming roles. When asked if he prefers playing a villain or a hero, Jim says, "I'll take the hero every time."

During the filming of *Ordeal*, a 1973 TV movie, Stacy went through an experience that seems funny now, but was harrowing at the time.

"On this particular day of shooting, I had to have a .38-caliber pistol in my hand. So I thought I'd bring my own .38 that I had. I took the precaution of unloading it. We get out to the desert, and I pointed the gun upwards toward the sky. And I say, 'Do you think we can use this in the shot, is this a good .38?' And they say, 'Yeah, it's fine. Is it loaded?' And I say, 'No, of course it's not loaded.' Then I put it in my bag in the back seat of the car.

"Ten minutes later we're surrounded by squad cars filled with cops with their guns pulled. It turns out this truck driver with a CB saw me holding up the gun, calls the police and takes down our license number. The cops pulled us out of the car and one shouted, 'You gotta gun?' And naïve me, I say cheerfully, 'Oh yeah! Here it is!' I then went to grab for it, the cop yells 'Don't touch that gun!' while he clicks the revolver back ready to shoot," laughs Jim. "It was so scary! We had to explain that we were from a production company. That halted production for a while."

In the late sixties and early seventies, Stacy's career was in high gear. Not only starring in the *Lancer* series but in films like *Flare Up* (1969) with Raquel Welch, *Heat of Anger* (1971) with Susan Hayward and *Paperman* (1971), a television movie.

One September night in 1973, a drunk driver sideswiped Stacy, who was riding his motorcycle with his girlfriend seated behind him. The girl was killed, and Stacy lost his left arm and leg. The accident, devastating both physically and emotionally, brought his career to a halt—temporarily. Stacy's life savings were wiped out by the enormous medical bills. Jim's agent, Stan Kamen, who would come to be a very important person in his life, coordinated a benefit dinner for Jim. Frank Sinatra, Liza Minnelli, Sammy Davis, Jr., and Connie Stevens all entertained at the benefit.

"That dinner was really something. Everyone was there. I was very moved and happy to have that cash in my pocket," confides Stacy. "It carried me through until I knew exactly what I was going to do. I remember thinking, 'Why not a disabled actor? Raymond Burr plays someone disabled on *Ironside*.' I was thinking about whether I'd be wearing prosthesis . . . an arm and a leg or whether I'd be in a wheelchair. There were a lot of things to think about."

Stacy, as anyone might in that situation, contemplated suicide. At the time, he said, he could deal with death but not being maimed.

"I was considering suicide before I found out that I still had my genitals. I woke up after about three days in the hospital. I was thinking to myself, 'My arm is gone. My leg is gone. Sports are the only thing that'll take care of my pituitary gland.' When I realized that my genitals were still there, that everything was okay, I decided to go on and see what life would be like."

Stacy in the film *Posse.*

His first film, just a little over a year after his accident, was the western *Posse* (1975) starring Kirk Douglas. "Again, that was Stan Kamen who came through for me. He asked Kirk to change the character, the nemesis for the mayor, to a newspaper editor, which I could play."

When asked what it was like returning to acting after the accident, Stacy hesitates and then says, "Once the shooting on me took place, yes, I liked being in front of the camera. Before that I did a lot of sitting all alone in my office on the lot. For about two weeks, I sat alone in there. Bruce Dern was doing his scenes with the horses and everything. When they started shooting my scenes, it was fine. In the meantime, they couldn't get me out of my office. I wouldn't walk around the streets on the set—to save my shoulder, number one. I didn't have a wheelchair then.

"Finally Kirk came in and tore the whole office apart," says Jim with a laugh. He said, 'You bastard, you're getting out of this room!' While I was sitting on the chair in there, they carried my chair and put it in the middle of the street on the set. I sat there for like five hours. I like Kirk Douglas. He's a fighter ... and a good man," adds Jim with warmth.

One of Stacy's most memorable, powerful performances was in the TV film *Just a Little Inconvenience* (1977), which co-starred Jim's friend

Lee Majors, who also produced the film. Written by Ted Flicker, the film was about a man who lost an arm and a leg during the Vietnam War. Stacy skis in the film, an incredible physical achievement on its own, and gives an inspirational performance.

Jim is also on the board of the first ski school for the disabled, which was founded eight years ago in Southern California. Now there are also schools in Northern California and Colorado.

Not all the roles that have come Stacy's way since the accident are ones that he's willing to take on. He has great strength in his convictions, and if the disabled are shown in any way that doesn't ring true to him, then he won't do the role. This is the case with a recent *Golden Girls* guest shot he was offered.

"What I didn't like about that script was the fact that my character was being deceitful about his disability," explains Jim. "He was hidden behind a desk, asking a woman out on a date. She couldn't see that he was disabled.

"I had done that when I was first disabled. I'd flirt with a woman from across the room at a restaurant. Then I'd get up out of my chair, and she'd see that I was disabled. It's not right. So, I told the *Golden Girls* people that if she knew he was disabled from the beginning and accepted my date—that was fine. They said no, and I didn't do the show. The only way I would have had hidden the disability was if the character was a liar who was hiding something else . . . who wanted something besides the date."

Among Stacy's most recent roles was an episode of *Cagney and Lacey*, called "The Gimp," for which he was nominated for an Emmy Award. He was featured on six episodes of the TV series *Wiseguy* where he played a newspaper editor who sped around the office in his wheelchair, letting nothing stop him from the job he had to do. Jim has also had a role in the film *Matters of the Heart* (1989), and a cameo in *FX II* (1991) as a robot who has gone out of control.

In recent years, Stacy has spent much of his time writing and producing screenplays. He's just finished one project for Whoopi Goldberg, and is working on another called *Burbank After Dark*. Jim's brother, Louis Elias, is also a writer. He adapted the novel *The Dark Side of Love* into the television film *My Kidnapper, My Love* (1980), which starred Stacy and was produced by his Ragamuffin Productions.

"My brother is a great writer. He started out as a stuntman. I remember he was on the set, and they gave him a job doing a stunt. And that was it. He got $125 and said, 'This is the business I want to be in,'" laughs Jim. "He was a stuntman during a time when stunts weren't even organized."

"In real life, Jim has been married twice. He married his first wife,

Stacy in the TV film *My Kidnapper, My Love* (1980).

Connie Stevens, during the early sixties. He remembers their wedding as "a *big* wedding." The duo were the darlings of sixties' fan magazines. Stacy still speaks of Stevens with great affection. His second wife was Kim Darby, the mother of his daughter Heather, now also an actress. "I'm proud of her," he says about his daughter. "She's doing it (acting) on her own, no help at all. She's very talented and a strong girl—we've raised her that way."

When asked to offer words of encouragement to someone who might be going through a crisis, Stacy says, "There's an old Swedish proverb . . . 'Give us the gift to see ourselves as others see us.' People can interpret that any way they wish."

Connie Stevens

Series: *Hawaiian Eye*
Role: Cricket Blake (1959–1963)
Series: *Wendy and Me*
Role: Wendy Conway (1964–1965)

During the 1940s, in Brooklyn, New York, a little girl, like countless others, lived for the movies and dreamed of becoming a famous actress. Little Concetta Rosalie Ann Ingolia had the determination and talent to make her dream a reality. By the time she was sixteen, Connie had already begun her career as a vocalist with the singing trio "The Three Debs." This led to stage appearances, including a Broadway run in *Star Spangled Girl* and roles in films like *Rock-A-Bye-Baby* (1958) with Jerry Lewis, *Susan Slade* (1961) with *Hawaiian Eye* co-star Troy Donahue, *Never Too Late* and *Two on a Guillotine* (1965). By the mid–fifties, Connie Stevens was well on her way to fame.

If you were to use one word to describe Stevens — putting her obvious physical beauty aside — it would be "dynamic." This petite blonde dynamo seems to have energy to burn. And there's not one role you'll see her in where she looks even the slightest bit bored. She exudes an infectious good humor and zest for life in all of her performances.

"I think my humor came from my Dad," explains Connie. "When I went to the movies as a child, to fill up voids in my life, I was very lonely. I've never forgotten those lonely years. I know that people go to entertainers for escapism . . . to be entertained and to forget about their problems. We as entertainers have no right to bring our problems out with us when we go on stage. Petulant stars leave me kind of cold. I'm an entertainer. That's what I do. And it shows that I really like what I do.

"Actually, it kind of sneaks by sometimes when I'm trying to be serious. I'm always looking for the joke in everything," she continues with a laugh.

Some of teenage Connie's first non–entertainment positions included a job as a soda jerk at Rockaway Beach, New York, and a sales girl and theater candy clerk in Hollywood.

143

Connie Stevens

"I was forever creating," recalls the beautiful actress with a smile. "Instead of making hot fudge sundaes, I made up new ice cream dishes. Instead of selling dresses I was constantly redecorating the windows of the store, and I couldn't make change, so I'd disappear from my post at the popcorn stand to go inside the theater and see the show. A few of my bosses told me to try show business, which is what I really wanted to do anyway."

Although Stevens began her show business career as a singer ("Kookie, Kookie Lend Me Your Comb," recorded while she had a terrible cold, was a big hit for her) acting is definitely her first love. This multi-faceted entertainer still sings at the top casino nightclubs in Nevada, and her 1990 concert tour was a sell-out. Connie also does a lot of work for the USO, and has entertained the troops many times over the past couple of decades.

"I had always wanted to become an actress. When I was a child, I would go to the movies every Saturday afternoon for thirty cents and see fourteen cartoons, movie shorts and three pictures. I'd have my breakfast, lunch and dinner there. It filled up all those voids so many of us had, especially Brooklyn kids," she reflects quietly.

"My favorite actresses were June Allyson, Esther Williams and Ava Gardner. You had a three-way street with those ladies. . . . I love opposites. My two favorite actors were Robert Walker and John Garfield . . . two opposite ends of the earth. My favorites now are Jack Lemmon, Robert DeNiro and Vanessa Redgrave. It varies with the times.

"It's a funny thing about me and opposites—it even extends to my children. I like to say I have a chocolate and a vanilla. One's real dark (Trisha Leigh) and the other is blonde (Joely)."

Stevens is referring to her two daughters by singer Eddie Fisher. Both have followed their famous parents into show business careers. Like their mother, they both sing and act. Connie has recently appeared with her daughter Trisha Leigh in the New Line Cinema film *Jack in the Box* (1991).

The nostalgia craze, which began in the seventies with films like *American Graffiti* and television series like *Happy Days*, is still going strong, and has brought a few recent roles to Stevens. She starred in *Bring Me the Head of Dobie Gillis* (1988) as gorgeous but snobby Thalia Menninger, the role Tuesday Weld originated in the fifties. She's also had starring roles in *Grease II* (1982) and *Back to the Beach* (1987) with Frankie Avalon and Annette Funicello. In *Back to the Beach*, having changed very little since the sixties, alluring Connie tries to steal Frankie from Annette.

There has been talk lately of doing a *Hawaiian Eye* reunion TV movie where Stevens would reprise her classic role as fun-loving shutterbug and singer Cricket Blake. Although she'd appeared in several films by 1959, Cricket was the first role that brought young Connie stardom.

Many don't realize that Stevens is also a writer who has been penning screenplays for the past six years, including the proposed *Hawaiian Eye* reunion film.

"We've been trying to do the reunion film for some time," explains Connie. "Either we couldn't agree on the script, or different people were off doing different things. We finally got together, and Bobby Conrad said

to me, 'You write it.' So I did. Now the studio is changing hands so quickly, we'll have to go in and re-present the idea. Actually, I have five properties that I've written. As soon as I have a new series deal, I'll have those properties ready to go. One of the projects I've written, that I'm very excited about, deals with our American Indian roots, the Civil War and how immigrants became Americans," she adds enthusiastically.

Stevens, who is part Irish, Italian and Iroquois Indian, is also heavily involved in Project Windfeather, an organization which helps native Americans. The organization has fifteen native American students in college, and is looking to finance fifteen more this year. Connie's efforts have focused on upgrading the living conditions on native American reservations.

Although Stevens is best known on television for her role in *Hawaiian Eye*, she really came into her own as a comedienne in the series *Wendy and Me*, which also starred George Burns as narrator and the landlord of the building where all the characters lived. Connie played Wendy Conway, the daffy young wife of airline pilot Jeff Conway, portrayed by Ron Harper. Also produced by George Burns, the show had some similarities to the *Burns and Allen Show* of the fifties in that Wendy Conway seemed to be based on the Gracie Allen character. However, the younger, sexier Stevens played the role with a broader technique and made it her own. The only similarity to the Gracie Allen character was the number of hysterical situations one well-meaning, confused person could cause. Today, the show holds up and remains some of the best work Connie Stevens has done as a comedienne.

How does Stevens feel now about *Wendy and Me* and working with George Burns?

"Well ... sometimes it was difficult. Actually, I learned more from George in one year than I did any five anywhere else. He's a perfectionist, and he was so used to working with Gracie. I had a new style. I was a brazen kind of kid who was confident in who she was. He chose me because of that. And then Gracie died right in the middle of production on our show. Well, you can imagine—the poor man was just devastated. So, we (the show) took second place in his heart, and then it went by the wayside.

"But I think I did some really funny work on that show. Recently, as a gift, someone sent me all the shows on video tape. I haven't looked at them lately. I do remember there was one episode where I met someone from a foreign country, and went to an embassy. I just watched a little bit of that, and thought to myself, 'Gosh, I was just so loose and free to do

Opposite: Anthony Eisley, Connie Stevens, Robert Conrad and Poncie Ponce in *Hawaiian Eye.*

a wide kind of comedy—you know, slapstick.' I was just having the time of my life. I guess I was very confident at that time, and I was surrounded by people who let me experiment."

Wendy did some wacky things—like mistakenly inviting her father-in-law's classmates to her husband's college reunion dinner, which had some very funny results in "Jeff the Senior Citizen." In "Jeff Takes a Turn for the Worse," Wendy's husband thinks she's sick when she's actually volunteering at the hospital. Through the plot's events, Wendy ends up with amnesia (with Wendy it was kind of hard to tell)! Stevens gives a great comic performance in the old amnesia device. With another actress, it would not have had the same comic effect.

During the early seventies, primarily known as a comedienne, a singer and a dancer, Connie had one special role which showcased her dramatic ability in the television movie *The Sex Symbol* (1974). The film's plot was basically a thinly veiled biography of Marilyn Monroe, showing the pitfalls of stardom, and particularly what the label "sex symbol" can do to a woman who is insecure to begin with. Stevens brought just the right amount of intensity and tender sensitivity to the part, and her performance was critically acclaimed.

Does Stevens herself have a favorite role?

"I have yet to do my *Gone with the Wind*. However, like my life and the shows I do, it's a smattering. I like ten minutes of one film and five minutes of another. I think the last ten minutes of *The Sex Symbol* was among some of the best work I've ever done.

"Some of the most fun I've ever had was on a picture called *Palm Springs Weekend* (1963). I don't know what got on the screen, but I sure had a hell of a time making it," laughs Connie.

With her cascading blonde hair and youthful face, Stevens looks more than a decade younger than she actually is. She has launched her own skin care line called Forever Spring. Although she is still much in demand as an entertainer, enterprising Stevens found that she was bored during the time between singing engagements and film and television roles. Rather than relaxing by the pool, or just lending her name to a line of cosmetics for a percentage of the royalties, Stevens became totally involved in almost every aspect of her own skin care and beauty products. She has a say in everything from the ingredients to packaging and marketing.

"About three years ago, I was asked to endorse some products that I felt weren't really that good. I started making suggestions like 'add this,' or 'take out that.' My business partner said, 'You seem to know a lot about this. Why don't you create your own products?' That's how I got started in the business.

"One of my primary concerns with Forever Spring is that we use

Stevens, Caroline Kido and Moko Mokusho in a 1964 episode of *Wendy and Me*.

natural ingredients," continues Connie. "My other concern is the preservatives systems used by larger firms with well-known brands, that ship all over the world. The products then sit in warehouses for years. They need eight to ten years of preservatives in order to stay good. The public doesn't realize that. I think the preservatives negate some of the effectiveness of the products."

While Stevens was a starlet at Warner Bros., she noticed that all the stars would sneak in to see a beauty expert named Louise Long. Long had a machine that retrained facial muscles, making lines disappear.

"It was huge, and looked like something out of Frankenstein. Later, I decided that I wanted to make this machine hand-held and battery operated. It's now one of our most popular items, and I feel responsible for making it the first American hand-held unit. It's been used in beauty spas all over the world for a few years now.

"Actually, I've become more health conscious since I started this business . . . practicing what I preach, so to speak. I've been eating a lot more fruit and vegetables and avoiding junk food. I used to grow my own vegetables. I had everything from melons to string beans by my pool. You could swim by and pick a string bean," laughs Connie.

Since her daughters have followed her into the limelight, would they be interested in going into the skin care business as well?

"They're concentrating on their acting careers right now. And their boyfriends, new cars and decorating their apartments. They don't have time for Mom these days," says Connie with a laugh. "Actually the skin care business is a nice business for a female to be in. And they've been around it for a long time, so I think through a natural evolution of things they'll get involved. They come up to the office once in a while and answer the phones. They use the products and know a lot about them—so perhaps someday they'll become involved."

Looking over the list of accomplishments of Connie Stevens, it's easy to see why she was once voted "Most Likely to Succeed" by her classmates in Brooklyn. She obviously gives her all to everything she does, and her two daughters should be very proud to follow in their famous Mom's footsteps.

Deborah Walley

Series: *The Mothers-in-Law*
Role: Susie Hubbard Buell (1967–1969)

A woman of many talents, Deborah Walley has always been involved in something artistic from the time she was a little girl—whether it be writing, dancing, ice skating or acting. Today she runs her own company, Lion Heart Enterprises, where she produces and writes family-style films with positive, optimistic themes.

Deborah's parents were a renowned ice skating team, the Walleys, who spent many years with the Ice Capades.

"At first, I wanted to be an ice skater like my parents," recalls Deborah. "And I did skate with the show when I was very small. They would bring me out at the end of their act. My parents felt that education was very important. So by the time I reached school age, I could only skate with them while on vacations from school. I wanted to be a skater but my father was totally against it because he said it was a hard life. Then I wanted to be a dancer. I studied in New York and actually had an offer from the American Ballet, but my father put his foot down again because he said it was too difficult a life. So," she laughs, "I got my revenge!"

Walley did indeed get her revenge by becoming one of the most popular young leading ladies of sixties' teen films such as *Gidget Goes Hawaiian* (1961), *Ski Party* and *Beach Blanket Bingo* (1965), as well as the Disney films *Bon Voyage* (1962) and *Summer Magic* (1963).

"I think when I got hooked on acting, I was already doing it. I was still a teenager when all of this began, and it was a natural progression. I did some modeling as a pre-teen, and when you're in that world things just sort of happen. My grandmother had a big house on Nantucket Island, and I had the opportunity to work in a theater there and got my equity card when I was twelve. I guess I got 'bit' then. I also went to the American Academy of Dramatic Arts, which I enjoyed very much," says the Connecticut-born Walley, who still gets back to New York about once a year to "recharge my batteries."

While at the American Academy of Dramatic Arts, Walley went on

Deborah Walley

stage, both on and off Broadway, in such varied productions as *Charley's Aunt*, Chekhov's *Three Sisters*, Shakespeare and musicals.

Her stage work led into early television guest shots on series like *Wagon Train*, *Playhouse 90*, *The Naked City*, *Burke's Law* and *Route 66*. In retrospect, her role on the *Route 66* episode "Ten Drops of Water" is the one she remembers with the most fondness.

"I had so many really wonderful experiences. I got to work with some incredible people, like Claude Rains on *Naked City*. I guess *Route 66* is the one I remember the most. It was a great part. The script was about a brother and sister whose parents had died," she recalls. "They were very poor, and trying to survive out in a desert environment during a drought. And, of course, George Maharis and Martin Milner come driving along. We filmed the show in Utah because, as you might remember, *Route 66* was a road show.

"I remember that when I interviewed for the part, they asked me if I could wrestle a calf. And I said, 'Of course, can't anyone?' She laughs. "Needless to say, coming from New York, I'd never even seen a calf! That was a special show to me, because it was in the very beginning of my career in film. It was one of the first shows that I did."

Walley went from being a successful but not widely known actress on television and stage to becoming an overnight sensation when she received the title role in *Gidget Goes Hawaiian,* which co-starred James Darren. Walley feels that she was, for the most part, typecast as Gidget after that film. One of the side effects of that sudden fame was becoming a popular fan magazine cover girl. The onslaught of publicity she received during the Gidget period was tremendous. Did Walley find it fun or intrusive?

"A little bit of both," Deborah admits. "It was overwhelming because the fame part virtually happened overnight. I had been a working actress, still a teenager, when suddenly I was receiving all this attention. People were 'Miss Walleying' me all over the place. They were practically scraping the floor and kissing my feet. It was more than just a little strange."

Walley, uncomfortable with extreme adulation as a teenager, today finds a little recognition "very flattering."

Deborah's favorite film role was as the gourmet cook/drummer/auto mechanic "Les" in *Spinout* (1966) with Elvis Presley. Les was a tomboy role, and Walley's buoyant comic style lent itself perfectly to this non–traditional, "one of the boys" female role.

"*Spinout* may not be the most outstanding thing I've done," she admits, "but it is the role I've enjoyed the most. I mean, I have done dramatic roles. Of course, Chekhov and Shakespeare were wonderful and challenging. Actually, it's very difficult for me to compare the satisfaction from doing a piece on stage to one on film.

"Norman Taurog was my favorite director in film. Harry Master George is my favorite stage director. Comedy is my first love, and I had so much fun making *Spinout*. It got great reviews. I'm really proud of my work in that film. The *New York Times* said that it was me that separated that film from all the other Elvis Presley films. I have my bathroom wallpapered with that review," Deborah jokes.

"Actually Norman Taurog and I had worked together before on a picture for AIP called *Sergeant Deadhead* (1965). It was a fun picture that didn't do very well, It was cute for its genre. Norman wrote the role in

Spinout expecially for me. The part was originally supposed to be for a guy. He changed the script so I could play the role.

"Anyway, when I knew I was going to do this Elvis picture, I thought to myself, 'I've never been a big Elvis fan. He really can't act. This is going to be a challenge.'" Deborah laughs at the memory. "I had all these pre-conceived ideas about Elvis not being very bright. He proceeded within the first day of filming to shoot down every pre-conceived notion I had about him. He was extraordinarily intelligent and very stimulating. We developed a very tight relationship—a platonic relationship—which I understand from hearsay was very unusual for Elvis and some of his leading ladies. We became very close friends, and we were pretty much inseparable during the shooting.

"I got to know him very well. Elvis was going through a very spiritual period in his life at that time. Not that it wasn't a thread that carried throughout his life. We stayed in touch for a while. Later, our paths went in two different directions and we kind of lost touch. Elvis was for me on a spiritual level a major turning point in my life," she confides. "He took me to the Self Realization Center and started giving me books. Our relationship was based on a student/teacher thing. It seemed like he almost wanted to cram everything he knew into my head. So, we discussed, what seemed to me, some pretty far-out ideas at the time. Our friendship really affected me and my outlook, and preceded some major changes in my life.

"I really know only my little part in Elvis' life. So as far as I'm concerned, he was fabulous and wonderful, and I loved him. I don't want to hear any of the negative stuff," Deborah says, referring to sensationalistic biographies of the legendary singer.

Following her role in *Spinout*, Walley was cast as Susie Hubbard Buell in the situation comedy *The Mothers-in-Law*, which starred Eve Arden and Kaye Ballard as the mothers-in-law and longtime neighbors. These two women gave interfering in-laws new meaning. One of the scripts actually had the meddling in-laws going along on their children's honeymoon! Directed by Desi Arnaz, the series was reminiscent in some ways of *I Love Lucy*, with the two women getting involved in hare-brained schemes much in the same way that Lucy and Ethel had sixteen years earlier.

Eve Arden portrayed Walley's mother, Eve Hubbard. Much to the character's dismay, her son-in-law, Jerry (Jerry Fogel), repeatedly referred to her as "Mother Hubbard." Kaye Ballard played Kaye Buell, Jerry's mother. Arden's sardonic delivery and Ballard's slapstick approach blended comically and balanced one another.

Had another actress portrayed Susie, she might have been over-shadowed working with talents like these. But this was not the case with Deborah and her uninhibited comic style. Walley was also a great crier on

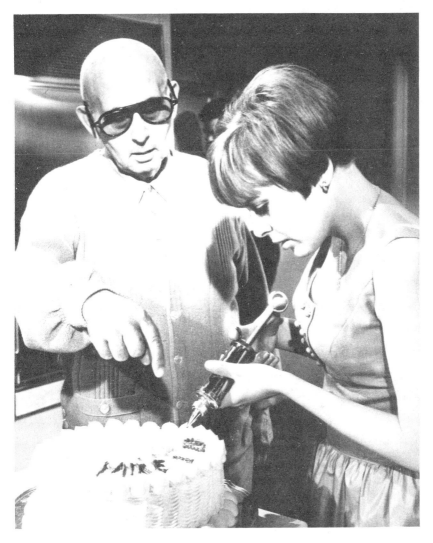

Norman Taurog directing Deborah Walley in *Spinout* (1966).

that series; you could enter her in the Lucille Ball Sweepstakes for loud, comic crying. In her character's frustration, with all the extensive meddling in her life, she often had to scream, "MO—THER!"

Walley says when the role on *The Mothers-in-Law* came around she was at the beginning of what would become a disenchantment with show business.

"Well, to be honest, the series came up at a time when I was starting to burn out," she admits. "I didn't really have any desire to do a television series. It came up and I did it. It was a great experience, I have no regrets. It was wonderful working with Eve Arden, Kaye Ballard and everybody on the show. We were very tight.

"Eve Arden was great . . . an absolute master. Desi Arnaz, let me tell you, could be difficult to work with, because he was truly the passionate Cuban that you might imagine. But when it came to three-camera comedy, no one knew about it like Desi Arnaz did. I mean, he started it. It really was wonderful working with him.

"The show was such a well-oiled machine," she continues. "It was my only series, other than a slew of guest appearances on other shows, that I've ever done. My biggest involvement with television is that show. We were very unusual in that I only recall one show, in the whole time we did the series, where we ever had to do something over again. We filmed the show live in front of an audience just like a play. Desi would never stop to retake something if the audience was there. And if there was a screw-up, after the audience left, then we'd do a retake. That happened once, *only once*, during the entire run of the series because most of us had a theater background.

"I remember that we were all sitting around a table in a restaurant scene. We were all supposed to be out to dinner together. And Desi said, 'Action!' And all of us picked up our tea cups at the exact same moment! And being aware of this we were all sitting there sort of posed — the cups in the same hand, in the same space — it was like the Rockettes," she laughs. "And I think it was me, actually, who started laughing. It became one of those contagious things . . . we all just couldn't stop laughing! And we actually had to stop and start all over again. That was the one and only time anything like that ever happened.

"It was a beautiful two years. I do love television. As a matter of fact, the film I'm producing now, *Good Medicine*, might spin off into a television series."

Deborah did continue a relationship with her TV mother, Eve Arden, after the series ended.

"Well, of course, you know that Eve passed away. I did keep in touch with her. And while I was living in Los Angeles," says Deborah (whose home base is now Arizona), "after her fall, I'd go over to Eve's house, while she was recuperating. We'd have lunch together once a month, sometimes more often than that, and just visit.

"This was a period when I was starting to back-pedal. I was pregnant with my youngest son, Justin, and I moved out to the mountains in Malibu. I really didn't want anything to do with the business. We lived a good hour from town. I pretty much spent time with my family and nature. Basically, I've lived my life like that ever since. That's why I moved out of California. Los Angeles was infringing on my mountain wilderness. So I haven't kept

A publicity shot of Walley from *The Mothers-in-Law*.

up with people as much as I sometimes would have really liked—other than a few people I was really close to."

It was during this period in Walley's life, after the television series, that she became more involved with her writing. She was planning to take a sabbatical. Deborah had worked very hard ever since she was a teenager and just wanted time "to be a mother."

"For a few years there, that's all I did. I played in my garden, and I was just 'mommy.' Pretty soon, the creative part of me started crying out. I began to write again. Actually, when I was a kid I used to write short stories and poetry. I wrote a book for my parents when I was thirteen. Though my mother says I wrote things long before that. But I *remember* writing the book. My mother, of course, has it preserved," laughs Deborah heartily.

"Writing was always a hobby. I started a children's theater with the man who is still my partner to this day, and another friend of mine. We called it Pied Piper Productions. I began to write scripts for the children's theater, and found that it was becoming a growing love. And then I started developing screenplays and other things. One thing led to another, writing to producing, and that's what I've been doing ever since.

"Producing is the only way I can get something happening just the way I see it . . . to retain creative control of the project," explains Walley. "I'm producing the film *Good Medicine* here in Arizona. *The Last of the Blues* is an animated project we will soon be getting off the ground. It's kind of a 'Bambi Beneath the Sea' about a family of blue whales."

Walley is committed to making wholesome family films which have an enduring appeal. Her greatest influence in this endeavor is Walt Disney, for whom she made two films as a teenager.

"I was under contract to Disney for many years," Deborah remembers. "Fortunately, in the beginning, Walt Disney was still alive. I did a picture with Fred MacMurray and Jane Wyman called *Bon Voyage*. We shot most of it in Europe. Part of the film was shot on the S.S. *United States* crossing. So we spent five days aboard that ship. Walt came along, which was fairly unusual. During that trip, I developed a very close relationship with Walt. He was a tremendous influence on me. He's really like my patron saint. Everything I've done in recent years, such as the children's theater, projects done in the children's market and family films, relates to that experience.

"It's so much easier to raise money to do a slasher film or a steamy sexual film than it is to get a G-rated family film off the ground. And yet there is a huge market for family films. Every time one comes out it does well. I remember one of the things Walt told me, he said, 'Animation projects and good family films are like a piece of real estate. They grow in value and have a long shelf life.'

"Disney would always wait for a few years, then re-release. And they're doing that still to a certain extent, although now they are also releasing the films on video. You constantly have a new generation of kids. You'll be selling *Jungle Book* just as easily twenty years from now, but can you say the same about *The Terminator*? Probably not."

Walley's older son, Anthony, is a director, and her younger son, Justin, plays guitar in a rock and roll band and is an artist. So both of her children have a love for artistic endeavors.

An early love of theater, her friendship with Walt Disney, acting in family films and motherhood all have combined to make Deborah Walley the caring filmmaker and writer that she is today. When she looks back on the days of her teenage stardom, she says:

"It seems now in retrospect to be a kind of dream. I've distanced myself from it. I have really changed horses. It seems like this is one person here, and that's another person there. And I love the one that's here now. The other one wasn't so bad either, but this one is a lot wiser."

Ray Walston

Series: *My Favorite Martian*
Role: The Martian, "Uncle Martin O'Hara" (1963–1966)

Ray Walston is a master at portraying characters that are larger than life ... somehow superior to ordinary mortals. Even if the character he might be playing isn't a supernatural one like a devil or a martian, you get the impresson that he knows something that you don't. This distinguished veteran of stage, film and television, with that knowing gleam in his eye and his dry, satiric humor, has given many a memorable performance. No one can deliver a comically caustic line the way that Walston can.

The Southern-born actor, who is either from Laurel, Mississippi, or New Orleans, Louisiana ("I always juggle the places of my birth and the dates, so no one is ever sure," he says), began his stage career in the late thirties. When did he first realize he wanted to become an actor?

"I think I was about six or seven years old. That's an interesting question that used to always be asked by Ruth Gordon. It always interested her how actors became attracted to acting," Walston explains. "In her case, her grandmother used to take her to the theater every Saturday in Boston. She fell in love with the theater and fell in love with acting. In my case, I was in New Orleans when I was very young. There were a couple of companies which put on one new show each week. I used to go to that when I was little, and I think that's where I fell in love with acting on the stage."

There are no actors or artists in Walston's ancestry. "I'm the only one who showed any interest whatsoever or any talent for the theater in my family," he says.

Walston, who has great knowledge regarding the theater and early Hollywood, mentions three idols from his younger days.

"I really fell in love with Spencer Tracy's work when I was young, and watched his career grow and grow. He had such a wonderful screen technique. There was also an actor in silent films — Emil Jannings. He was a brilliant, brilliant actor. I admire actors whose names you don't even know or hear of today. Strangely enough, there was an actor that Paramount brought over from Budapest, Hungary, his name was Paul Lukas. He was a big hit on stage in Hungary. Paramount gave him a seven-year contract only to learn he hardly spoke English at all. The studio tried to buy out the contract for a quarter on the dollar. He steadfastly refused, and began to work very hard to learn English. He did some excellent films. Later on in his life, he won an Academy Award for *Watch on the Rhine* (1943). I got to know him, and liked him very much."

Although he has done many wonderful roles on film and television, Walston is essentially a stage actor down to the very core of his being. He uses stage rather than film terminology, and refers to the theater constantly when talking about acting. He is most definitely a purist when it comes to the stage.

"There is no comparison between stage and film," he says emphatically. "Once the rehearsal period is over and the out-of-town tryouts have been completed and the show has opened in New York—then the actor is in control. You don't have to be concerned with what is going to be cut out of your work. In terms of movies and television, when it is all put together you don't know what you'll lose or what you'll keep. Also there is the factor of the live audience. Now a lot of actors say that is the wonderful part of stage. It is, but often it can be a problem because of long runs. I've been in a few long-running plays. One lasted two years, another two and a half years, one production lasted one year and so forth. Obviously, you can't be in the best of health for that long a period of time. Things happen to human beings, and you've got to rise above whatever does happen to you when you're on stage. You have to get out there and do it. Sometimes it can be quite tough but most of the time, it really is quite a lot of fun."

Walston made his stage debut with the Margot Jones Players of Houston, Texas, in 1938. He stayed with that particular troupe, which did twelve plays a year, until 1943. From there he went to the Cleveland Playhouse, which he says is "the finest regional theater in America. It was a wonderful, wonderful training ground. That was a very professional outfit, so that when I arrived in New York in 1945, I had a solid foundation."

While in New York, Walston appeared in *The Front Page*, *Me and Juliet* and two of his biggest hits both on stage and in film—*South Pacific* and *Damn Yankees*.

As the bossy, cranky devil, Mr. Applegate, in the film *Damn Yankees* (1958), Walston didn't use any of the stereotypical props one might use to play a devil. You won't find any horns, red suits or pitchforks. Walston does more with nuances—such as a raised eyebrow, diabolical laugh or mischievous gleam in his eye—to convey the comic evilness of the character than could ever be done with obvious devices. The only physical reminder that the character is a devil is the subtle touch of red he wore, such as red socks or a red tie.

A publicity shot of Walston from his 1986 TV series *Fast Times.*

Walston has a couple of marvelous musical numbers in the film, including "Those Were the Good Old Days," as the devilish Applegate remembers his part in all kinds of atrocities in the history of the world. Also, in the scene where he gets angry at his sexy assistant Lola (Gwen Verdon), he does a hilarious parody of Verdon's number "Whatever Lola Wants."

Tab Hunter, Gwen Verdon and Ray Walston in *Damn Yankees* (1958).

Walston won the coveted Tony Award for his superb stage performance in *Damn Yankees*. The actor says the Tony Awards didn't have quite the same prestige in the mid–fifties that they do today.

"At that time, in 1955 and 1956, they wrote you a letter two months before the ceremony, informing you that they were going to give you the Tony Award. They expected you to show up at the ball," he recalls. "When I got the letter, I thought, 'Well, that's nice.' It didn't have the notoriety that it does today. Winning it today . . . it looks better. At the time I won the award it was just a piece of silver with the two masques of the theater on it. There was something written on the back of it about Antoinette Perry, the lady director. The element of surprise was gone. Now, I understand that it's like the Academy Awards. The nominees don't know who is going to win it."

The actor is pleased about how the stage version of *Damn Yankees* adapted to film.

"The picture was a true representation of the Broadway musical we did, because of the fact that when Warner Bros. decided to do the film they brought the entire cast out from New York, with the exception of the leading man. They gave that role to Tab Hunter simply because of the fact that they had one picture left on his contract. They wanted to get it over with, and cast him in the movie. I think, to their surprise, he turned out very well."

Walston was not as pleased with how his role as the shirtless, tattooed Luther Billis in Rodgers and Hammerstein's *South Pacific* carried over from the stage to screen. This tough-guy role was a departure from the impeccably-dressed, witty characters that Walston usually plays.

"When they adapted the script for *South Pacific* (1958) for the screen, they cut down the part I was playing rather drastically," he remembers. "Only through conniving and other means—while we were shooting the film—did I persuade the director, Josh Logan, to the point of where he not only put aspects of my character back in, but also added various other elements as well. However, it was chewed up when the editor got a hold of it. Some things were lost."

Following his roles in *Damn Yankees* and *South Pacific*, Walston acted in such early sixties films as *Tall Story* and *The Apartment* (1960), and *Convicts 4* (1962). He also had an interesting role as Lana Turner's compulsive gambler chauffeur in *Portrait in Black* (1960). Still, when one thinks of Ray Walston during the sixties, his martian character from the TV situation comedy *My Favorite Martian* immediately comes to mind.

As the martian, he displays some of the delightful comedic aspects of his earlier devil character. The 450-year-old martian was arrogant and irritable. He merely tolerated earthlings. And you can't blame him, really; we all did seem somewhat dimwitted in comparison to him. Human beings were always misinterpreting the martian's actions—accusing him of being a spy or of trying to kill himself by jumping off a building (when all he really wanted to do was get some oxygen). But as crusty as the martian was on the outside, there was a soft heart deep down inside.

One of Walston's first lines in the pilot episode, "My Favorite Martian," immediately clues the audience in regarding the type of character they would be getting to know. The martian emerges from his spaceship, much to the shock of Tim O'Hara (Bill Bixby), and says, "What are you waiting for me to say—take me to your leader?"

Bixby's charming if somewhat naïve character adopts the martian as his uncle. He becomes, forever after, "Uncle Martin." The two actors had a marvelous chemistry together. Walston's superior, wise demeanor and Bixby's innocence complemented each other well.

The martian was a fascinating fantasy series character. He could read minds and levitate objects with his finger. He also became invisible when he sneezed, had no fingerprints, and later had his own time machine.

Walston has fond memories of his co-star, Bill Bixby.

"I enjoyed working with Bill Bixby. That was his first show, and he was really quite wonderful," says Walston. "I really think that without him and that particular style of work he was so good at . . . I don't think the show would have worked without that. He is really such a wonderful light comedian. Of course, his career has changed since then. He's gone on to do some dramatic roles. However, in *My Favorite Martian*, he really stood out in charming, light comedy."

Walston recalls that his schedule on *My Favorite Martian* was a grueling one.

"Regarding enjoying doing the show . . . I can't say, 'Hey, everything was great and I had a wonderful time,' because it was tough and rough," confides Walston with candor. "We did, at that time, thirty-eight shows a year. We did the shows without rehearsals. At that time, only a few shows were done on tape. One was *The Lucy Show*. I don't think any of the other shows were done with one camera. In those days, the way we did most of the situation comedies, was to come in on Monday, read it, and maybe block a little bit. Tuesday, we came in and blocked the whole show. We shot the show on Wednesday, Thursday and Friday. There was no luxury of rehearsals because we filmed the show in just three days. If we finished one episode at 3:30 in the afternoon, they'd thrust in our hands the script for the next episode. And we started to work on the new show right away.

"As a matter of fact," he continues, "this morning I was just thinking of the last week of the first season. I don't know how or why the thought came into my head. I remember that my mind was so exhausted that I could hardly remember anything. You see, the martian had some very long speeches. Bill Bixby would say, 'Why?' and I would deliver a half-page speech. And he would say, 'Where?' and I would deliver another half-page speech.

"At the end of the first season, I went to my agents at the William Morris Agency. They were also the agents of the producer, writers and director. They put together the whole package," points out Walston. "I went in to see them and told them how mentally exhausted I was. They said, 'Aw, don't worry about it. We'll get this worked out.' I said, 'The only way you're going to work this out is to write the show differently.' They said, 'Nah, what we'll do is get you a tele-prompter.' And that's what they did. They got a tele-prompter for the second and third season. For the majority of the episodes in the second and third years, I was reading off of a tele-prompter."

The special effects on *My Favorite Martian* were among the best in sixties fantasy series. Much of it was done not by trick photography, but by using various mechanical devices, including a transistor which made the martian's antennae go up and down.

"At first, it was very awkward. They had a motorized piece of equipment strapped to my back. There was a wire running down the arm inside of my coat sleeve and shirt. I would push the button and the antennae

Bill Bixby and Walston in a scene from *My Favorite Martian*.

would go up and down," elaborates Walston. "At the beginning, they would cut holes in all of my clothes to get the straps through to strap the device on. Then, as we went along, it was developed to a better degree, where we had a guy who would kneel, holding this piece of equipment against my back. They would shoot me from the waist up. Offstage there was this remote control switch. That's how they did it in the later episodes."

Some of the actors in this book have told some funny stories regarding animals on the set of their shows. Sixties sitcoms used animals fairly often. Ray Walston had a terrifying experience with a chimpanzee on his series which truly illustrates the dangers of using wild animals, who can be extremely unpredictable, for entertainment purposes.

"It was in September of 1963. September can be the hottest time of the year in Los Angeles. On that particular day, we were shooting a scene in a convertible car outside," recalls Walston. "Bill Bixby was driving and I was sitting next to him. The chimpanzee was sitting directly behind Bixby. It went berserk. And instead of going forward and grabbing Bixby, it reached over and grabbed me. It pulled me back and practically pulled me out of the front seat into the back seat of the car. He had me over the front seat and was chewing on my face and hands. Nobody was moving. Nobody moved, and for forty-five seconds, this beast was chewing me up. Bixby was sitting there. Everybody was stunned. The only way I got away from him was to get my hand, open the front door, and throw myself out feet first. By this time, I was covered with blood. I had on a gray suit and it was absolutely red. Production was down for seven or eight weeks. I had to have plastic surgery. I have many scars left from the experience.

"I put my foot down thereafter, and said 'No more animals!' During the third season, they actually came up with a script that had a lion in it," he continues incredulously. "They said they were going to get a lion with no teeth and no claws. They said that I shouldn't worry, that it was a real pussycat! I said, 'Well, suppose the pussycat you're talking about gets playful, leaps upon me, pushes me over and I get a concussion of the brain or something?' They said 'All right, okay, never mind.' They changed the script so that Bixby was involved with the lion instead of me. Much to Bixby's horror, the day they shot the scene with the lion, the entire camera crew was encased in a steel cage! Bixby was very disturbed about it. At any rate, there will be no more animals for me. I refuse to work with them."

Walston has not stayed in touch with his former co-stars as much as he might have liked.

"When I came from Broadway to do my first picture in 1957. . . . Well, at the end of the film, I had to learn that people just don't stay in touch. It's over. You try and keep in touch but you don't. It's very difficult to do, and it's one of my greatest disappointments. Now there are exceptions, of course. At this moment, Bill Bixby lives twelve or fourteen blocks from me. I never hear from him, but I do run into him on the street once in a while."

In recent years, Walston has gone on to do many other character roles in several films and television series, including the role of Mr. Arnold Hand in both the film (1982) and television series (1986) versions of *Fast*

Times at Ridgemont High, as well as a 1979 series called *Stop Susan Williams*. He also played the devil again in the pilot for a TV series entitled *Satan's Waitin'*. The actor feels that his characterization of the martian has been a double-edged sword. People love the character; however, he feels he has become too identified with it.

"It used to bother me a great deal to be recognized as the martian," admits Walston. "I've gotten to the point where it doesn't bother me anymore. I'm a very slow-minded person. It took me four weeks into the production of *My Favorite Martian* to go to the producers and say, 'Wait a minute. I'm in a position where I can ruin my career as an actor with this sort of baloney with antennae coming out.' They said, 'No, no, that won't happen.' I think the show has ruined the career of a very promising actor. You become associated with a certain character. Now the fact that he was such an outlandish character made it worse.

"Audiences know you as the character you portray. They know you by the character's name. Whether it's Uncle Martin or Archie Bunker—it doesn't matter. And I dare say that during the entire run of *All in the Family,* the American people knew Carroll O'Connor as Archie Bunker. Although I don't know him personally, I must say that I have great admiration for Carroll O'Connor. He beat the rap. He got the *Heat of the Night* series, put it together, and forcibly made a hit out of it. A lot of us have been unable to do that. We are held down by the association we made with some of the characters we've portrayed."

Walston has been a member of the Actors Studio since 1949, and enjoys acting and directing the Los Angeles branch of the studio—the Actors Studio West.

"I keep myself alive by going over there, doing scenes or directing once a week," he says, "I don't work once a week, but I do go to the sessions. I watch the actors at the Actors Studio and listen to them . . . their methods. I invariably end up with the thought, 'Where is the skill to do it on a stage?' The only way an actor can get skill and technique is to be in front of an audience on the stage. I've always felt that these young actors in Los Angeles are here because they want to be film or television stars. Because if they want the theater, the theater is in New York. You cannot develop technique unless you are coping with an audience in a play continually," advises Walston. "You cannot do that and not learn something."

Ray Walston seems to be continually learning, and has a deep respect for his craft. Obviously, the theater is more artistically fulfilling for this passionate actor. However, thanks to the magically enduring qualities of television and film, his colorful characterizations will live on indefinitely.

Dawn Wells

Series: *Gilligan's Island*
Role: Mary Ann Summers (1964–1967)

Of all the castaways on *Gilligan's Island,* Dawn Wells has received the most fan mail. As sensible and sweet Mary Ann Summers from Horners Corner, Kansas, the radiant brunette captured the hearts of TV viewers everywhere. Wells still receives about 300 or 400 fan letters a month and says, "Everybody has something kind to say. It's nice to know that you've made a difference somewhere."

Most of the characters on *Gilligan's Island* were exaggerations—the pampered movie star Ginger Grant, played breathlessly by Tina Louise; the lovable bumbler Gilligan, played with childlike charm by Bob Denver; the fabulously wealthy Thurston and Lovey Howell, portrayed with great comedic style by Jim Backus and Natalie Schaefer; and the good-natured if sometimes hot-tempered Skipper played by Alan Hale, Jr. Only the Professor (Russell Johnson) and the level-headed, optimistic farm girl Mary Ann were down to earth, like people you might meet anywhere.

A small point, but Mary Ann was the only person on the island who was appropriately dressed for the beach. Ginger wore long, satin evening gowns; the men were all clad in long pants; Mrs. Howell was dripping in diamonds; but Mary Ann wore shorts and cool little crop tops. In fact, the sixties censors were more concerned with Dawn Wells than with Tina Louise (who played the sex symbol) because Dawn's clothes were more revealing. "Like Barbara Eden, I couldn't show my navel," laughs Wells.

"I was very much like Mary Ann," says the likable actress with a sunny disposition. "She was in essence me."

This wholesome beauty's parents were not actors; however, Wells remembers that her grandmother was an artistic person.

"My mother's mother, my grandmother, composed music, painted and could sew anything . . . she was a real artist. She died when I was thirteen," Dawn says with tenderness. "She was the only one in the family that I can think of that had a real creative talent. I'm really sorry that she didn't live to see me become an actress, because I think we would have had a lot in common."

Wells' original ambition was to become a ballerina, not an actress.

"I studied ballet for about twelve years and then I developed trick knees—knees that dislocate. I had to quit dancing altogether. So when I went to school, I never took any theater at all. I was a debater and speaker," recalls the Nevada-born actress, who is a great believer in higher education.

"When I attended Stephens College, my alma mater, a women's college in Missouri, I took a theater course sort of like you might take a P.E. course . . . it was an outlet. I was a chemistry major, as a matter of fact. Dr. West, who was head of the department at that time, and my adviser talked me into changing my major. Stephens College was a two-year college at the time, so I transferred from Stephens to the University of Washington in Seattle because of their theater department, and in order to get my theater degree."

As a little girl, Wells never once entertained dreams of becoming a famous actress.

"That was something that never entered my mind," she says emphatically. "And I really didn't even, in quotes, want to be a 'movie star.' I said I'd give myself one year to become an actress. If I didn't actually make a living as an actress during that year, I'd go on and do something else. And I really chose Los Angeles over New York because at that time, New York was mostly musical comedy and I don't sing. So, I thought, what are the odds of working if you don't sing? I chose Los Angeles just thinking that maybe I'd get a job there. Today there are many places you can go to earn a living as an actress, like Dallas or Chicago. In those days, it was just New York and L.A.

"Looking back, I was really very lucky. I was very well trained. Stephens College and the University of Washington provided a terrific training ground for me. I was a perfect ingenue type. And I think because I was well trained, when I later auditioned for parts, I was hired because I was capable of doing the roles."

Dawn was Miss America in 1960, but she does not feel that winning the title helped her in her acting career in the least.

"The Soroptimist Club was my sponsor for the Miss America Pageant. They really sort of talked me into doing it," she remembers. "The reason I decided to enter the contest was because I thought it would be a good experience for me to get up in front of people. I wanted to see if I could retain my composure in front of an audience. I had no idea that I would win, and had no illusions about being a beauty queen. When I first went to Los Angeles, people would ask, and I would tell them that I was a Miss America. I always thought the title was more of a hindrance than a help, because producers tend to think of you as pretty but not well trained. You know, an awful lot of people come to Los Angeles to be movie stars because

Dawn Wells

they are beautiful, without thinking that you have to have a background in acting too. So I just stopped mentioning 'Miss America.' I'm not saying anything negative about the pageant, but I didn't think it was a help to me as an actress."

Upon arriving in Hollywood, Wells was immediately put under contract at Warner Bros., where she did guest appearances on *Bonanza,*

Wagon Train and *Burke's Law*. The next year she was cast on *Gilligan's Island*. How did her parents feel about her success?

"My dad has been gone a long time. He died during the last year of *Gilligan's Island*. I don't believe either one of them wanted me to become an actress. They were very pleased, at least, that I was successful and not out of work." She laughs. "I think that's what most parents worry about!"

Today, Wells seems delighted at the enduring success of *Gilligan's Island* in syndication. The program is broadcast several times a day on cable television as well as local stations.

"We are one of the longest running shows in the history of television, we've never been off the air. And I cannot go anywhere without someone recognizing me. I mean, I got on a plane coming out of Disneyworld a couple of years ago and the whole plane started singing the *Gilligan's Island* theme song," Dawn says with a laugh. "I was up in Bavaria in the mountains on a German tour with a friend of mine who speaks German. This whole tour was in German. Suddenly these people came running out of the woods in the rain shouting, 'Mary Ann! Mary Ann!'"

And in a tale that seems to come right out of a script from *Gilligan's Island*, the actress remembers traveling to the Solomon Islands by canoe with five women from Stephens College. They slept on the floor in huts with no running water or electricity. A tribal chief's wife on one of the remotest of islands recognized Wells from her TV portrayal. "You can't escape it no matter where you go!" she laughs.

Does she enjoy the recognition?

"Oh, sure," Dawn answers. "Do you know why? *Gilligan's Island* holds such a wonderful place in everybody's heart. The critics hated it, but everybody has a favorite episode. Everybody has a story that they remember. Two or three generations have gone by, and the show is part of everybody's childhood. It's kind of nice to be a part of television history, I think. You know you could just go into oblivion, and you could find something much more memorable artistically, supposedly . . . but nothing that has meant so much to so many people."

When asked to recall a behind-the-scenes story from the show, Wells relishes the memory of an episode entitled "Feed the Kitty," which involved Gilligan and a lion.

"You know, Bob is so tall and skinny—he's just this wisp of a person. Well, he had this episode with a lion. We were trained all week about what to do with this lion. When you have to get up and run away from the lion—they actually ask you to ease away for a step or two, before running, so that you don't startle the lion and make it want to come after you. They also told us not to make loud noises. If we were to scream, we were just to open our mouths and dub the scream in later. We'd been working all

Dawn Wells as Mary Ann in *Gilligan's Island*.

week with this lion, and Bob Denver wasn't afraid of him at all. As a matter of fact, he wanted to pet the lion. And the trainers kept saying, 'But really pet the lion. Don't just stroke him. He'll think you're a fly and take off your hand.'

   "The lion just had a rope around its neck and would saunter around sluggishly all day. But at about four or five o'clock, he would start waking up because his natural instinct is to hunt at night. And it was the last shot of the last day on a Friday night at about nine o'clock. By this time, the lion was pacing around.

"In this last scene, Bob was to come into the hut. Three walls of the hut were, of course, the real hut but the fourth wall was where all the cameras were," she elaborates. "Bob was supposed to come in and think the lion was chasing him. He would board up the door and the windows and then sit on the bed and turn around and relax. He was to realize that the lion was on the bed and then jump up to get out the door.

"They put the lion on the bed and then got ready to shoot everything. Bob came in and boarded up the doors and window, sat down on the bed, and then jumped too quickly, like he was not supposed to do, and with that the lion sprang for Bob. Bob only had eight feet to run, and luckily the two twin beds the lion was resting on were not attached together. So when he went from one bed to the other they scooted apart and the lion lost his balance. The trainers were able to get to the lion after that.

"The funny part was Bob's reaction," she adds with a laugh. "Bob turned around with a karate chop. He was actually going to defend himself against a *lion*, which I just thought was so funny! I have a home movie of this, as a matter of fact. I would have been a puddle of butter, I'm sure, if I had been in Bob's place. You tend to think because you're working with these wild animals that they're little pussycats, but they're not!"

There were a couple of episodes of *Gilligan's Island* where Wells was featured as the main character. One was the "The Postman Cometh," in which the men on the island find out that Mary Ann's fiance in Kansas has married another girl. In order to soften the blow, all the men romance the pretty young girl. Wells' reactions at the men's sudden ardor are hilarious.

In "The Second Ginger Grant," Mary Ann gets hit on the head and wakes up believing she's the glamorous movie star. Her parody of Tina Louise as Ginger is nothing less than hysterical. This episode gave each actress a chance to play the other's role.

Gilligan's Island was cancelled while still very popular with audiences. A scheduling conflict regarding *Gunsmoke* and *Mannix* is blamed. Since the cancellation, a couple of animated series based on *Gilligan's Island* and three reunion TV films have been produced. Wells remembers that the reunion films were a lot of fun to do.

"We were cancelled after we had taken a hiatus, and we even had the scripts purchased for another season," she recalls. "There was a political reason behind the cancellation. So, we never had a chance to do a final episode and say good-bye to each other. Twelve years later we came back to do the first 'rescue' film, and it was as if we had stopped on a Friday and started again on a Monday. Everybody just sort of fell into place."

Sadly, since Jim Backus, Alan Hale and Natalie Schaefer have passed away, there will be no more reunion films. Wells has some lovely things to say in tribute to her fellow cast members who are no longer with us.

"I think the best thing I can say about Jim Backus is what a kind and giving man he was—especially as a comedian—because an awful lot of people don't share their souls. Jim was so generous about giving you hints, suggestions and help. It was my first series and there was a lot for me to learn. He was very giving with his knowledge, and that doesn't happen very often. He really was a very nice man.

"Alan Hale was probably the dearest soul to walk the face of this earth. He was the same size as my father, so every time Alan hugged me it was like hugging my own father. I never saw him cranky, and I never saw him have an unkind word for anyone. Over the years, we did a lot of personal appearances together. It was really something to walk right behind him into a room, and to watch people's faces light up when they saw him. Alan never met a stranger. He shook hands with everyone and called them by name. He was just a joy.

"And Natalie was one of those people that is really one of a kind. She broke the mold. There aren't any Natalie Schaefers coming up. She was very much like Lovey Howell. We were extremely close. She had no children, and I think I became a kind of surrogate daughter to her. As a matter of fact, I talked with her the day before she died. We saw each other probably twice a week, and I spoke with her just about every day.

"The show has gone on so long, you think we're all going to live forever. You look at yourself twenty-five years ago, and think we're all going to be around indefinitely. Russell, Bob and I just came back from a personal appearance in Baltimore about a week after Natalie died. It was so good for the three of us to be together, and kind of relive it all. We haven't seen Tina very much. She's not on our 'bad' list or anything, we just haven't seen her. She didn't do any of the specials. She hasn't been around to experience this with us.

"It was a real joy to be part of a company that loved each other. Our producer, Sherwood Schwartz, is a very kind man. He's a good soul and a wonderful family man. To have an experience with your first series . . . you hear about people who don't speak on the set and that sort of thing. There was none of that with us. I think that's why it transferred to film so well. People can feel that love."

In the years since *Gilligan's Island*, Wells has been quite busy with a variety of endeavors, including a couple of national stage tours, teaching dramatics at Stephens College and Purdue and writing and co-hosting the Children's Miracle Telethon for the state of Missouri. Certainly one of the most significant things Wells has been involved with is designing a Velcro clothing line called "Wishing Wells" for elderly and disabled people.

Wells explains how she became involved in designing the clothes.

"I had a dear friend who was in a nursing home for eleven years. And because of the Children's Miracle Telethon I became very close to a young girl with cystic fibrosis who underwent a lung and heart transplant. I spent 180 days with her at Stanford. Missy would be in intensive care and she'd have to wear these flour sack hospital gowns. She'd say, 'God, can't you give me something with color?' And because I'd costumed myself on stage so much, I thought, 'You know this Velcro is great for quick changes. Why can't we do something where from the front a person looks like they're completely dressed, but in the back's it's all one piece that comes together?'

"So I worked very hard on it for about five years. I'm working on it still constantly, there's a lot yet to develop. This is also wonderful for people with arthritis who can't manipulate buttons. I get maybe fifty or a hundred letters a month at my office about my clothes saying, 'I knew Mary Ann would come up with something nice like this.' I keep thinking if I had been a bitch on a soap opera, I wonder if they would have cared." She laughs heartily. "You know, you have to stop and think about that because Mary Ann's image is so nice. People have such a fond feeling for her, which I think is really interesting."

Also a comment on Dawn's positive image is the fact that many families will come to see her again and again when she tours with plays across the country.

"I played one theater in Florida ten times. I always feel that they'll come and see me the first time just to see what Mary Ann looks like in person, live on stage," she theorizes. "I think a lot of actors make a mistake by doing the same play 10,000 times—thinking people will just come to see them in person. I feel that you've got to give an audience a good product. If they come out saying, 'Wow! I had a good time. Gee, I didn't know she could do that!' They'll come to see you again."

The role Wells considers her favorite was Beatrice in *The Effect of Gamma Rays on Man-in-the-Moon Marigolds*.

"I loved that part because it was someone that no one would ever think to cast me as. Shelley Winters played the role in the movie. It was a real stretch with the gray wig, rollers, cigarettes and an old bathrobe. It was really the most creative challenge for me, because it was such a stretch."

Wells is also on the board of curators and is chairman of the alumni development committe of Stephens College, where she also teaches acting at least once a year as the guest artist in residence.

"I am very committed to higher education and to women's education. I raise money for the college because I think it so important that the college remain a female college, and that we provide something for women that a co-educational college can't. Because of my experience with Stephens, the president, Dr. Patsy Sampson, who is just a wonderful woman—I've become a real adventurer. I've done the gorilla mountain climb and took that trip to the Solomon Islands.

"I really feel very lucky about my life. I came from a strong family background," reflects Dawn. "My mother is still living and is a wonderful woman. Even though I came from divorced parents, I feel that I had two families growing up. I had steady family ethics and principles. My head was never swayed by 'show biz,' as they call it. And I think that's probably one of the reasons I've sustained. I've never been out of work except by choice since I started in the business. I think a lot of that is because I am strong inside, and never really got carried away with what everybody says. You need to set goals. It's a business like everything else, and you can't take everything personally all the time. I feel very fortunate, I really do. I like to try and pass that on to kids along the way."

Jane Wyatt

Series: *Father Knows Best*
Role: Margaret Anderson (1954–1960)

Audiences everywhere recognize Jane Wyatt as the sweet, under-standing mother on the long-running television series *Father Knows Best*. However, this beautiful actress has also appeared in over thirty theatrical films and numerous stage productions.

Never was her beauty more artfully showcased than in the master-piece *Lost Horizon* (1937). One scene of Wyatt's remains particularly memorable, and not one line of dialogue was uttered. Ronald Colman follows her on horseback to a cascading waterfall and flower-filled pond, where he catches a glimpse of her swimming. Glistening with water, with a warm glow in her eyes and a radiant smile, Wyatt is nothing less than breathtaking. In addition to looking beautiful, Wyatt, who was in her twenties at the time, played the part of Sondra with a maturity and grace way beyond her years.

Lost Horizon still holds up today as one of the greatest motion pic-tures ever made. The script by Robert Riskin captures the essense of all religions ... the common thread uniting them all. This Frank Capra classic was most definitely ahead of its time.

The film, partially disintegrated, was recently restored by the Ameri-can Film Institute, using the original audio and black-and-white stills. In an early morning interview, I asked Jane, fresh from planting and watering out in her garden, if she approved of the restoration.

"I thought it was wonderful. They had a premiere for the new re-stored version at the Chinese Theatre. I attended with Frank Capra and his wife. The theatre was absolutely packed. I thought the film looked beautiful at the Chinese. I prefer it on the big screen, I don't like it on the little screen at home," says Wyatt. "The film is so universal, this longing for utopia, and it put a word in the English language—Shangri-La. I think Franklin D. Roosevelt was the first person to use it when he christened the aircraft carrier 'Shangri-La.'"

One thing Jane vehemently disapproves of is the colorization of films. "They should leave films the way they were meant to be. *High Noon*

Jane Wyatt

would never be the same in color," she says firmly. "It's funny though, I think when you start looking at black and white you completely forget that it's not color. It doesn't seem to bother you. When I watch *Father Knows Best* it never occurs to me to think, 'Oh dear, it's not in color.'

"I had to watch some episodes recently for a marathon we (the cast) got together to do for the Family Channel. I was surprised at how good that show really was. It teaches children about the basic truth in life and the difference between good and bad. It doesn't hit you like a sledge hammer, and it's an entertaining half-hour. At the end of the program you have something to think about."

Prior to her film work in *Lost Horizon*, Wyatt was in a few films, including *Great Expectations* (1935). However, most of her training and acting experience was on the stage. Born into one of America's oldest families, Jane is the daughter of a drama and music critic and an investment banker. She made her Broadway debut after spending two years at Barnard College.

"My mother was a dramatically inclined person; she wrote plays for which she won prizes, and was a critic for *The Catholic World* for thirty-five years. My father's ancestors came to America about the same time the Dutch bought Manhattan from the Indians. There are towns in northern New York named after my family," explains Jane, who is obviously proud of her family heritage.

Since she is from a historic family, I asked Jane if her family was shocked by her decision to go on the stage. "No, they didn't make a fuss about it. My father came from a long line of ministers — four uncles, a great-grandfather and a grandfather. When I went on the stage, my father said, 'It doesn't worry me, she's doing the same thing they've all done, only she's going on the pulpit of the stage,'" says Jane in her distinctive New England accent. Jane says she is still recognized today, and often times it's because of her voice. "The minute I open my mouth, and people hear my voice — that's it," she says with a laugh.

Since *Lost Horizon* was one of her first films, I asked Jane if Ronald Colman, a seasoned pro, was helpful to her. "He was absolutely charming, a lovely person and a poet. Ronnie was delightful, and so nice to me. He was never condescending, and gave me all sorts of pointers on what to do and what not to do. I liked him very much.

"All those big stars I played opposite of, like Ronnie Colman, Gary Cooper, Cary Grant and Robert Young — they all were dedicated actors. They arrived on the set fully prepared, there was no playing around or acting starry. They would just get on with the job, and they'd interplay with you. Bob Young always handed it to you on a silver platter. They knew how to support the other actor. I was crazy about each and every one of them, and admired the way they worked," remembers Jane with fondness.

Some of Jane Wyatt's notable theatrical film roles include *None but the Lonely Heart* (1944); *Boomerang* (1948); *My Blue Heaven* and *Our Very Own* from 1950. In *Our Very Own* Jane played the mother of three daughters, Ann Blyth, Joan Evans and a very young Natalie Wood. Her warmth and understanding in the part of the mother were harbingers of things to come — in her most famous role, Margaret Anderson of *Father Knows Best.*

Father Knows Best was an extremely popular television situation comedy which ran from 1954 until 1960. For three consecutive years, Wyatt won the coveted Emmy Award as best actress for her outstanding portrayal. *Father Knows Best* has been shown in syndication almost constantly since it stopped production more than thirty years ago. For two years after the show ceased production, reruns were shown in prime time.

"*Father Knows Best* was different than most of the other situation comedies in that we rehearsed on Mondays," recalls Jane. "We shot not for three or four days but *five* days on a half-hour script. That's unheard of. Also, all our scripts were finished before we started. All thirty-nine scripts were completely prepared before we started the season. Now you go and act in a TV episode and they're still giving you pink pages while you're standing on your feet before the camera. The extra time we put into the show is one reason that I think it's been popular this long with viewers."

Jane Wyatt as Margaret Anderson was at once perceptive, proper and loving, and she had a wonderful sense of humor. She was always ready with a shoulder to cry on, an encouraging word and praise for her children. Her character remains one of the most beloved sitcom mothers on television. Jane was very busy with her own family and professional engagements, yet she still found some time to spend off the set with her television children—Elinor Donahue, Billy Gray and Lauren Chapin—according to series co-star Robert Young.

"I was never terribly close to the children as people; as the characters they played, yes," explained Young during The Family Channel's Father's Day marathon. "I think Jane was closer to them personally. She was genuinely interested, and made it a point to ask them how their day or week-end was. As a result, they naturally felt closer to her. Jane had a real maternal attitude towards the children."

Jane says of her fellow *Father Knows Best* cast members: "We all got on very well with each other. We weren't sloppily attached to one another, we didn't think of ourselves as a family off the screen. They were three very professional children who were all put on the stage very young. We had respect for each other as colleagues. I'm still in touch with them. Bob and I talk on the telephone quite often. I see Elinor quite a bit, she's prettier than ever and works all the time. I knew Billy the best because he was about the same age as my own boys. Lauren had a rocky time of it for a while, but now things have turned around for her. She has two very nice children, and is a minister in Texas."

Wyatt's character of Margaret Anderson was a great supporter of the underdog, as was shown in several episodes of the series. Anyone—not just family members—who needed a helping hand was sure to get it from Margaret. She helped an old, retired author get the recognition he deserved

The cast of *Father Knows Best*. Left to right: Lauren Chapin, Elinor Donahue, Robert Young, Jane Wyatt and Billy Gray.

in "Spaghetti for Margaret." In the episode "Margaret's Other Family," she helped a poor furniture maker and his family. Margaret also helped an Hispanic gardner, Fronk, adjust to the American way of life in "Margaret Hires a Gardener."

Decades before "Ann Romano" from *One Day at a Time* went to college with her daughter, Margaret did the same thing with her daughter

Betty. She had ESP (translated as woman's intuition) in "Margaret's Pre-monition." Margaret had strong ethics. In "Dilemma for Margaret," she was supposed to give a speech to the PTA about how to raise children. Since her own daughter had recently had trouble with a prank at school which ended in vandalism, Margaret decided she wasn't qualified to give the speech. These episodes illustrate that fifties sitcom mothers weren't quite as backwards as stand-up comedians would have you believe.

In real life, Jane married Edgar Ward in 1935 and has two sons of her own. Michael has taken after the artistic side of the family—he became a pianist. Jane's other son, Christopher, is the treasurer of a company called Hexell in San Francisco. Jane also has three grandchildren. Did either of her sons ever show an interest in the acting profession?

"Absolutely not," says Jane. "I don't think they even bothered to look at me on television. I know my husband doesn't. During the years *Father Knows Best* was on the air, they would watch the show and say, 'Oh, there's Mom.' Then they would go on and concentrate on the child closest to their age."

Wyatt was a working mother in an era when there were very few women with careers.

"It's not easy," explains Jane. "I was lucky enough to be able to have very good help at home, and I had a wonderful husband. By the time I was working on *Father Knows Best* one of my sons was in boarding school. The other was going to school right near the house. It all seemed to work out. I think a mother has to give up a lot of things for her children, cer-tainly on the weekends. You don't do anything except do things with the children. I did wonderful things with my sons. The youngest one always wanted to go to concerts because he was a musician. The other one wanted to go to baseball games, which I didn't care for, but I struggled along," she adds with a laugh. "We went to museums, on expeditions, and camping. We really concentrated on the children during the weekends."

In her leisure time Jane enjoys gardening and bird-watching. "I'm a big gardener. I garden like mad. I also love to look at birds. I go off with my little group of friends and we spend a night here or there and we watch for birds.

"I also love to travel. I recently took a trip to Lima, Peru. All the hostesses on the plane recognized me from *Father Knows Best*, although I was hardly dressed like Margaret Anderson. I was wearing a camping outfit. I love the movies and the opera as well. I'm involved with the March of Dimes. I've worked with them for a long time. I was the first woman national trustee. I've just been rolled off the board, now I'm honorary. I still go on long tours for the March of Dimes."

In her career since *Father Knows Best*, Jane has been in several films including, most recently, the NBC-TV movie *Amityville*, where she played

Patty Duke's mother. "I didn't know *Amityville* would be a horror film before I read the script, I thought it would be about the Civil War," explains Jane with a laugh. "I loved my role in this picture because I'm not playing the nice, good person I always play. I'm not really bad, I'm critical in this film. On *Father Knows Best*, I was never critical. I loved working with Patty Duke, she's a marvel as an actress."

When asked what she would still like to do in her career as an actress, Jane says wistfully: "The stage is absolutely my first love. *Father Knows Best* was my big hit on television, certainly *Lost Horizon* was something to be proud of as theatrical films go, but I've never had a really outstanding New York/Broadway play. I've been in many fine productions of plays by Somerset Maugham, Clifford Odets, and Lillian Hellman, but never a real stand-out."

One thing is for sure: Jane Wyatt is a stand-out in the minds of countless film and television viewers. There's no doubt that she will do whatever she sets out to do — and do it well and with style, just as she has throughout her exceptional career.

Dick York

Series: *Going My Way*
Role: Tom Colwell (1962–1963)
Series: *Bewitched*
Role: Darrin Stephens (1964–1969)

A sensitive and perceptive artist, Dick York did not always have things easy in his life. It's a well-known fact that there is a fine line between tragedy and comedy. A sense of humor helps people deal with pain. Perhaps this is one reason York was such a brilliant dramatic and comic actor. Watch any of his performances and you see a rare depth mirrored in those big, brown eyes. No one could ever have accused Dick York of giving a hollow performance—there's always subliminal emotion beneath the outward characterization.

A deeply spiritual man who tried to find the beauty in all aspects of life, York devoted much of his time in recent years to helping the homeless. Even though he was ill for decades with emphysema and a degenerative spinal condition (he was injured during the filming of *They Came to Cordura* in 1959), Dick still found the strength to raise money for sleeping bags, food, clothing and even an AIDS clinic for the homeless.

Illness may have cut his acting career short, but it did not break his spirit. Despite everything, York was a cheerful man. He laughed and made others laugh.

"If you see somebody hungry, it would be nice if you gave them something to eat. If someone is cold, it would be nice if you covered them up. As long as it is that easy—we'll just do it, I guess," said Dick, in our interview less than one year before his death.

Even as a small boy, Dick wanted to help people. He said that acting was actually a third choice for a career. He added that he would have much rather gone into a career such as medicine or law. York said it was the nuns at his Roman Catholic grammar school in Chicago who first noticed his talent.

"I must tell you those nuns saved my life. Thank God, I had a few

189

Dick York in the mid–sixties.

nuns along the way who were bright enough to look at me and see the potential," commented Dick.

When asked if any of his own five children showed an interest in acting, he replied:

"I believe all children act. I actually do believe that I had my childhood with my children. We used to go on picnics in our living room, and on hiking expeditions together. They are wonderful, patient, kind people. I've learned a lot from them. I do think it's impossible for children

A 1965 photo of York and his five children. From top to bottom: Kimberly, 12; Stacie, 9; Christopher, 5; Matthew, 4; and Amanda, 10.

to grow up around actors without learning how to act, because actors are acting all the time. I don't know why we do that. I think it's because we really have no idea who we are. We don't really know what persona to be. We read a lot, and see who we would like to be. And then we go and pretend to be those people in our games as children. And then one day, somebody turns to you and says, 'We're doing a play.' And all of a sudden, you find yourself up on stage. In my case, I was dressed in a bear suit. I played the father bear in "Goldilocks and the Three Bears." The costumes were courtesy of some wealthy lady who paid for them. Some nuns saw something in a little boy in kindergarten that nobody else saw."

From school productions Dick went on to join the Jack and Jill Players.

"Some nuns heard me sing, and they said to my mother, 'Gee, Mrs. York, he's got a beautiful voice.' They said they knew a music teacher who could teach me," remembered Dick. "The music teacher had enough wisdom to say, 'You have a beautiful voice, but we'll wait until your voice changes before we train you. In the meantime, why don't you go to dramatic school where you can practice being in front of an audience.'

"So we went and I auditioned for the lady. I told her that I couldn't pay," confided Dick, who remembers being so poor as a child that sometimes his family had to live on just gravy and bread. "The lady was so impressed by my acting talent that she said, 'If you lay the carpet, paint the scenery and clean up, we'll take that as your tuition.' She didn't offer me a scholarship, but she said I could pay for my lessons by working. She knew that people from the slums don't want to take something for nothing. This lady allowed my mother to keep her pride, so she wouldn't have to refuse my lessons. And that's also how I got into radio, from the kindness of people who believed in me. I began to audition for people, and they started hiring me, and kept right on hiring me."

During the thirties, Dick began acting on radio in Chicago. He was on *That Brewster Boy*, and played Billy Fairfield on *Jack Armstrong, American Boy* for six years. He also began his writing career as a young boy when he both wrote and acted in a show called *Junior Junction*. "We did write a show called *Junior Junction*. At that time, it was called *Teen Town*. It was written by and for teenagers," he remembered.

While a teenager working in radio, Dick met his wife, actress Joan Alt. The coupled married in 1951.

"My wife Joey (his pet name for Joan) was twelve when I first met her. I was fifteen. She came to AFRA (American Federation of Radio Artists), they didn't have the 'T' for television then. I inscribed a photograph to her, it read 'To Joan, Love, Dick.' Later she added a message to what I had written. She wrote under the 'To Joan,' 'To the most beautiful girl in the world. I'll love you until the day I die.' She was only twelve then. Honest to God, she's the snottiest girl I've ever met!" he joked. "I remember when I introduced her to Gene Kelly. I said, 'Gene, I'd like you to meet my wife, Joan.' And Gene said, 'Oh, Dick. She's not ugly at all.' And Joey said to him, 'I thank you very much, Mr. Astaire.' I mean she's really something else! Gene Kelly laughed and laughed! He's my hero. I couldn't dance the steps, but whenever Gene Kelly danced, he was dancing for me. Joey can't dance either. That didn't prevent us, when we were kids, from going over to her house after seeing *Slaughter on Tenth Avenue* and trying to dance that dance! We waltzed all over, throwing each other up against the wall. It was wonderful. We've been playing like that ever since."

After working on radio in Chicago, Dick moved to New York, where he continued acting on various radio programs. Word got around town about his talent, and he was asked to audition for a role in the Broadway production of *Tea and Sympathy*. York was nominated for the New York Drama Critics' Award for his exceptional performance in the play.

"I'm glad somebody," he said, "had enough courage to hire a radio actor for *Tea and Sympathy*. I remember when we opened with the show. We went to a party at Elia Kazan's house. Everyone was reading the notices. Humphrey Bogart and Lauren Bacall were walking in the door-way . . . it was wonderful . . . and just one of those things where a twenty-five-year-old boy opens in his first Broadway play. I remember somebody tapped me on the shoulder, I turned around, and it was Fredric March. He said, 'Excuse me. I'd like to introduce myself. My name is Fredric March, and I wanted you to know that you did a brilliant job in the play. I really enjoyed it.' Imagine that, an actor of Fredric March's stature," said Dick incredulously about the man with whom he would later act in the film *Inherit the Wind*.

York's next big break on stage was the role of the naïve yet aggressive cowboy Beau in *Bus Stop*. He took over the role from Albert Salmi.

"It wasn't so much fun replacing somebody, even though I had been the one they had cast in the first place. My wife never liked me in that part," he laughed. "She said, 'You're not that way.' And I said, 'Which part am I not?' And she said, 'You wouldn't grab a girl and throw her over your shoulder.' And I said, 'I would if that was the only way I could get her! I'd pretend to be anything if I was really hung up on the girl.'

"The only thing we had to change was to cut the word 'virgin' in Boston. God, have things come a long way since then. It's when Beau turns to the girl and says one of the sweetest lines in the whole play. He says, 'I'm virgin enough for the two of us.' Well, I guess I just have one of those simple, kind of sweet faces. You don't believe . . . no matter how rowdy the character was, that there was a bad bone in his body. When I said, 'I'm virgin enough for the two of us,' the audience just went crazy! Because it looked true," he added, laughing at the memory.

The major film role in York's career was as Bertram T. Cates, the young high school teacher who defied the law by teaching Darwin's theory of evolution in the classic film *Inherit the Wind* (1960). Though soft-spoken, Cates stands up for his beliefs. As Gene Kelly's cynical reporter character (based on H.L. Mencken) says to Spencer Tracy's lawyer character (based

Donna Anderson, Dick York and Gene Kelly in a scene from *Inherit the Wind* (1960).

on Clarence Darrow): "There's only one man who thinks in this town at all, and he's in jail."

York gave a performance of great range during a jail scene in *Inherit the Wind*. An angry mob of townspeople are singing and burning an effigy of Cates outside the jail. Without uttering a word, York shows the character's mounting frustration as he peers through the bars at his small-minded neighbors. It is a beautiful piece of acting.

York actually wrote the speech in the film where Cates explains the theory of evolution to his students.

"Stanley Kramer said, 'Hey, you know what this guy is all about, don't you?' I said, 'I think so.' And he said, 'Why don't you go ahead and write the speech to those kids.' And I did," said Dick with pride. "Kramer used to invite everyone to the daily rushes. He'd tell us, 'If you see anything there that you think you can do better, we'll do it over.' I mean, the man wanted quality, he wanted it to be *right*.

"I enjoyed making that film tremendously. To work with Stanley Kramer, Mr. March and Mr. Kelly—it was incredible. For one thing, they all waited for two weeks for my baby to be born in New York. Joey never wants to have the babies, she just wants to carry them forever. They went in and induced labor but Chrissy wouldn't be born. I had Spencer Tracy, Gene Kelly, Fredric March and Stanley Kramer all waiting for the birth of my baby. And they say Hollywood doesn't care? They're nuts! Two weeks later, I blew in on the set, and we rehearsed the whole film. Kramer shot it like a television show with four cameras. Remember that long courtroom speech of Spencer Tracy's—the one where he cross-examined all the witnesses? That was all done in one take! Isn't that remarkable? It was just incredible. Everybody gave him a standing ovation."

Spencer Tracy was not well during the filming of *Inherit the Wind*. York remembered that director Stanley Kramer was sensitive to the issue of Tracy's health. "Stanley said, "We don't care. Whenever you feel well enough to shoot that scene—we'll shoot it.'"

Dick also remembered that there was one scene between himself and Spencer Tracy where Tracy was distracted.

"I got his attention," remembered York. "Every once in awhile, an actor reaches down and says, 'This other actor isn't listening to me. He's dismissed me. He's playing the scene by himself, and I'm not going to let him.' I demanded that Spence look at me for that scene. And he did. Something happened between us as actors—it was great.

"I also remember that we had a problem with billing. My agent told me that Florence Eldridge (Fredric March's actress wife) didn't know that I had a costar billing over her and over Donna Anderson. Florence was concerned about her billing, and that made Freddie concerned. I was asked to give up my billing to Florence. I said, 'I don't care. If I'm any good, they'll find me. If I'm not any good, they won't want to find me.' It seemed natural to me that Florence should get the top billing," explained Dick. "So Donna Anderson and I went on the card together, which was good anyway. What the hell is billing anyway? People in the general public don't pay any attention to it. They say to themselves, 'I know so-and-so was in that picture, and I knew I liked him, but I didn't know he had so many credits. I didn't know he'd been in radio for fifteen years, and on live television and all of that.' My entire life has been acting. And I really don't think I'm an actor, I think I'm a writer," added York, who wrote four screenplays.

Before his role in *Bewitched,* York did a lot of guest shots on various television programs, as well as a regular role on the series *Going My Way.* He was in a *Twilight Zone* episode entitled "A Penny for Your Thoughts," in which he played a meek bank clerk who temporarily had the power to read minds. He was also on episodes of *Route 66, Alfred Hitchcock Presents* and *Playhouse 90,* among other shows. *Route 66* and *Playhouse 90* were two of York's personal favorites as far as his television experiences. In *Playhouse 90,* he costarred with Paul Muni.

"Mr. Muni couldn't see out of one eye. He couldn't see the cues. He didn't know when the cameras were going to be on him," recalled Dick. "I told him not to worry, because he and I were going to be sitting together at the defense table. I helped him. Actors need to help one another, because if one person decides they're a star, they can make life so miserable for you. While the scenes were going on, I'd lean over and say, 'Muni?' And he'd say, 'Yeah?' I'd whisper, 'When the girl stands up they're going to have the cameras on you.' So we worked together as actors on that."

Certainly the most visible program Dick has ever appeared on is *Bewitched.* Out of all the actors on that show, he had the most interesting part, because his character, Darrin, was the one who had most of the spells cast on him by the various witches.

In so many of the episodes, he was able to take on character flaws such as vanity, miserliness or snobbishness and exaggerate them for comedic purposes. He could even demonstrate that too much of a good thing—complete honesty, or a perfect memory—could be disagreeable. In that respect, the role of Darrin Stephens had to be an actor's dream. And when done correctly, as York played the role, it was a joy to watch.

Dick's own affable personality came across in the role of Darrin. A consummate actor, York could go from manic fury to forgiving tenderness in seconds, which is particularly evident in his end-of-the-episode scenes with Elizabeth Montgomery. Montgomery and York had a sensual chemistry that was lacking in her scenes with Dick Sargent, who later took over the role of Darrin.

York was especially good in the verbal sparring scenes with his mother-in-law, Endora (Agnes Moorehead). And his gentleness shone in his onscreen moments with Aunt Clara (Marion Lorne). She was the only witch Darrin wouldn't get too furious at.

York had some especially funny episodes on the series. One was "A

Very Special Delivery." In this episode, uncharacteristically, Darrin is being insensitive to his pregnant wife. His mother-in-law sees this, and puts a spell on him to give him all the symptoms of being pregnant. He swells up, his back hurts, he craves pickles and starts crying at the drop of a hat. In this episode, Endora scored points for women everywhere!

York played the part of a pregnant man perfectly. He is not at all effiminate, but just acts as any human being would in that situation. No doubt York had a lot to draw on, since he and his wife were the parents of five children!

Thirty years later, Bill Cosby tried a dream sequence "male pregnancy" story on his normally well-written *The Cosby Show*, with disastrous results. The men on the show wore padding and made vulgar remarks about what orifice of the body the baby would emerge from. Cosby should have taken inspiration from "A Very Special Delivery," and York's classy interpretation, before allowing his writers to come up with that episode.

Usually on episodes of *Bewitched*, York would play through an entire episode with an exaggerated character flaw. In "Divided He Falls," he gets to play two sides of a personality in one episode, when he is split in two. One "Darrin" is a complete workaholic with no thought except that of business. The other "Darrin" is the world's most single-minded party animal who just wants to have fun, fun and more fun. Each aspect of Darrin was comically obnoxious without the other side to balance it out.

"People are making a fortune off that show," said York, who made no secret of the fact that the popular series was not a pleasant experience for him. Dick was in a great deal of pain, because of his back injury, during the filming of *Bewitched*. "It's shown night after night, day after day. I don't get a dime from any of that," asserted York. "What I do get is letters. People write asking for my pictures, which I can't afford to buy, and my autograph, which I can't afford to put a stamp on."

Did it make him angry that shows are rerun in syndication?

"No, the reruns don't make me angry at all. I'm grateful that they are still being shown, because that at least allows me to call the talk shows, and somebody will pick up the phone and listen to me. That way I can tell people how to help other people and they do it. It helps in my work for the homeless. Hell, if I was born into this world to just have a good time and screw people over, I suppose that's what I'd be doing. So I can't take any more credit for what I'm doing than what other people are not doing. I'm nobody special. Everybody is special. Everybody can do something."

Dick did what he could to help those in need, although he was frustrated with the red tape and bureaucracy that goes along with trying to help people as an organization. That's why he did what he could as an individual. "Do you think Mother Theresa asks permission from the pope

York as Darrin Stephens in one of the time-travel episodes of *Bewitched*.

every time she wants to feed a child or pick up a leper?" he asked. "She would much rather get the job done, and ask the pope later."

While philosophizing, York came up with a beautiful concept blending his work on *Bewitched* with the man he was.

"I believe there is a single molecule of light somewhere that dispels all the darkness. And if everything is silent, then you will hear the voice of someone laughing in the wilderness. Sometimes you have to laugh when you go by graveyards. And maybe that's what *Bewitched* is all about.

"People have said to me, 'I watched that show when I was recovering from multiple sclerosis in the hospital,' or, 'I saw that show when I had just gotten back from Vietnam and I needed something to believe in.' That love is the coin in which I am paid. The guy from Vietnam said, 'I wanted to believe in something. I couldn't believe in God because he let my friend die right in my arms.' If you couldn't believe in God anymore, then maybe you could believe in magic. And maybe circuses, clowns, magic and miracles are what's beautiful in this life. If you told me tomorrow that you had irrefutable proof that this life is all there is, I'd still go on doing what I'm doing — because miracles have to be done here on earth. They're not needed anywhere else."

Dick York passed away February 20, 1992.

Alan Young

Series: *The Alan Young Show*
Role: Host (1950–1953)
Series: *Saturday Night Revue*
Role: Regular (1954)
Series: *Mr. Ed*
Role: Wilbur Post (1961–1966)

Once acclaimed as the "Charlie Chaplin" of television by *T.V. Guide*, Emmy Award winner Alan Young is also a writer (six situation comedies and *Mickey's Christmas Carol*), a former cartoonist and commerical artist.

With a sincere smile and a mischievous glint in his eye, Young continually projects the witty aspects of his own personality into the majority of roles he portrays both in films and on television.

In the entertainment industry, Young is known to be as friendly as he appears in his television characterizations. George Burns, Alan Young's boss from the *Mr. Ed* series, says in his book, *All My Best Friends*, that Alan won the role of Wilbur because "I thought Alan was the type of man that a horse would want to talk to."

Alan Young was born Angus Young in North Shields, Northumberland, England. He was raised in Vancouver, Canada, and began his acting career at age twelve as a monologist and impressionist.

How did this career in show business come about?

"My sister was supposed to do something at a Scottish gathering, a recitation of some sort," remembers Alan. "And I don't know what happened but she couldn't do it. So I said, 'I'll do it!' I thought they might pay me. So I did it. I got up and imitated Harry Lauder and did a few silly imitations of English comedians. And they liked it. They didn't pay me, but they liked it."

In the record time of one week, following Young's first performance, he obtained a job on radio.

"I really enjoyed radio during the early days. In fact, somebody from that first party had his own radio show. He said he wanted me to do the

A 1951 publicity portrait of Alan Young.

same thing on the radio for him. So the next week, I was doing the same thing on the radio. *Then* they began to pay me," adds Young with a chuckle.

Since he started in the business as such a young boy, what comedy idols did Alan pattern himself after?

"When you're that young, you try and pattern yourself after the last person you thought was funny," says Alan. "I patterned myself after a great many English comedians that I thought were pretty funny, because this was in Canada and it was a British community that we lived in, and that's all we were around. Then I began to admire Jack Benny. I began to try and do his type of material, but I couldn't do that. I gradually found my own niche."

Alan Young found his own niche indeed, particularly with his variety program *The Alan Young Show*, for which he garnered an Emmy Award in 1950. In an age where broad, slapstick comedy ruled in the variety format, Young had a quiet, understated style—much like his idol Jack Benny, but with his own interpretation. Gags such as pies in the face, seltzer bottles and the like weren't as much of the norm on *The Alan Young Show* as they were on other variety shows of that period.

Perhaps if the shows had been preserved on film and put into syndication, Alan Young would be primarily known for *The Alan Young Show* rather than *Mr. Ed* today. Certainly the program was critically acclaimed and well received. Yet Young decided to leave the show before its fourth season. Why?

"It was live, and I could tell that you just couldn't keep the level of quality up live," explains Alan in his familiar, polished speaking voice. "There was no tape then, you just did it. You fell on your face or you lived. And I was also doing movies at the time. I could tell the technical quality of the show was going down. I wanted to put it on film the way George Burns and Lucille Ball were doing their shows. But the contract they had me under was just for live performances, so they didn't have to put the show on film. I thought to myself, 'This can't go on getting worse and worse.' I then made the decision to quit. Actually I enjoy revue (variety) the most ... it's more of a challenge ... because it's different characters and sketches. There's more variety with that format as opposed to situation comedy."

Following his radio work with the Canadian Broadcasting Company, Young served in the Canadian navy in 1946. He then went on to a film career that was not as successful as it could have been, given Young's considerable comic abilities. One of his early roles was in *Mr. Belvedere Goes to College* (1949) with Clifton Web and Shirley Temple. In that film, Young portrayed a completely obnoxious college student who torments uppity Mr. Belvedere. That role was a departure from the "good guy" parts Young is best known for, and he was hilarious in this change-of-pace role.

Aaron Slick from Punkin' Crick (1952), listed by at least one source as one of the worst movies of all time, may have thwarted Young's efforts at a major screen career. Decades after the movie was made, Dinah Shore, who also starred in the film, made quite a few jokes about it on her daytime talk show. Another early film in which you can catch Alan Young is *Gentlemen Marry Brunettes* (1955) with Jeanne Crain and Jane Russell.

Connie Hines, Mr. Ed and Alan Young in *Mr. Ed*.

Russell later recalled Young as "a very dear man." *Androcles and the Lion* (1952) was a good film which also did not do very well. Young says it was one of his favorite roles.

"In those days, it was two strikes and you're out in the film industry," Young once told author Richard Lamparski, "they didn't really take a third chance on you." In 1960, Young starred in *The Time Machine* (1960), which remains his favorite film role to this day and is shown fairly often on television.

Alan Young in the 1989 series *Coming of Age*.

Alan Young is best known for the fantasy situation comedy *Mr. Ed*, in which he portrayed affable architect Wilbur Post. Wilbur lives in a country home with his beautiful wife, Carol, played by Connie Hines. One of the most amusing things about the program was that Wilbur was always out in the barn talking to his horse and ignoring his curvy young dish of a wife. She would parade around in bathing suits—anything to get

Wilbur's attention. But if Mr. Ed called Wilbur on the phone, Wilbur was out the door. Hines brings plausibility and humor to a character who must either be jealous of a horse or be convinced that her husband is nuts. Deep down, she is both—but she loves the guy anyway.

Over the years, many jokes have been made about the *Mr. Ed* series. Surely the plot was far-fetched, although it was not as bad as *My Mother the Car*, which featured Ann Sothern supplying the voice of Jerry Van Dyke's deceased mother reincarnated as a car. *My Mother the Car* is an example of bad fantasy TV; *Mr. Ed* was good fantasy TV. Alan Young's honest reactions—not just as a straight man, but as a great comedian—make Wilbur Post a believable character. Without Young in the starring role, the show most likely wouldn't have lasted more than a season.

The whole premise of Mr. Ed *only* talking to Wilbur supplied quite a few funny plot lines. If you're watching an episode, the writing—especially Mr. Ed's harmless but sarcastic humor and witty comebacks—almost makes you forget that Ed is actually a horse. Close your eyes and he becomes a character like any other sitcom character. He's every bit as troublesome as the teenage kids or annoying in-laws featured on other situation comedies. Western actor Allan "Rocky" Lane supplied the voice of Mr. Ed. He was never given credit during the series' run. The producer must have wanted people to believe that Mr. Ed really talked. They must have figured (not giving viewers much credit for intelligence) that if the audience knew who supplied the voice, the magic would be gone. Lane deserves a good portion of the credit for the show's popularity. His delivery, phrasing and rich baritone voice *made* Mr. Ed. Lane passed away in 1973, and Mr. Ed died in 1979 at the age of thirty-three.

Larry Keating, formerly with the *Burns and Allen* program, and Edna Skinner portrayed the Posts' neighbors, Roger and Kay Addison, for the first few years of the program. Witty, urbane Keating as Roger was the perfect foil for Alan Young's character, while Edna Skinner brought a sassy quality to her role as Kay. (Skinner also played Maggie the cook in the television series *Topper*.) Both supporting players really shone in their roles. Sadly, Larry Keating passed away during the 1963 season. Edna Skinner stayed on a while but left after the 1964 season. Two new neighbors were brought in, Leon Ames and Florence MacMichael as Gordon and Winnie Kirkwood. Both are wonderful actors, but something was missing. Their chemistry with the other characters wasn't up to par with Keating's and Skinner's.

Young has fond memories of *Mr. Ed*, but had no idea the show would have such longevity. It has consistently remained a favorite in syndication, particularly with children.

"I think *Mr. Ed* was my favorite show. So, I presume that that character would be my favorite. Wilbur's a bit too much like I am anyway so I can't actually call him a role," muses Young. "I knew the show would be a hit. I was convinced it would be popular. But I had no idea it would go on and on like this. I get phone calls from my relatives in Britain now saying, 'You're back on the air again.' Kids watching the show are in the third generation of viewers, which is really incredible."

One of the funniest episodes of *Mr. Ed* was "Wilbur Post Honorary Host," in which Wilbur interviews Ed for a book on horses. Wilbur really gets into his work and becomes obsessed with horses. He even starts imitating a horse, neighing and crawling around on all fours. Of course, his wife and best friend walk in and see him and think he's losing it. Architect Wilbur is supposed to be working on building plans but is too involved with his book to do it, so they put him in an isolated room. It's some of Young's best comic work in the series.

Has Alan kept in touch with any of his co-stars from *Mr. Ed*?

"I haven't seen Edna since the show finished. She moved up north. I talk to Connie quite often. My wife and I, and Connie and her husband, get together for dinner quite often. After the show ended, Connie decided to get married and raise a family. She married a man with children, and she raised them. That's been her big joy in life," says Alan fondly.

Young retired from show business for a brief period in the late sixties to become a Christian Science practitioner. But happily for audiences, he later returned to the entertainment industry.

In addition to acting, Alan also does voice-over work on several popular cartoons. You can hear him regularly on *Duck Tales* as Scrooge McDuck ("my second favorite role," he says); *The Smurfs*; *Fat Cat* and *Mr. T*.

Two of Alan Young's four children have chosen careers in the performing arts.

"My son, Cameron Young, was a stand-up comedian for a while. Then he decided to become an actor, and has done an awful lot of commercials. Now he's decided to get behind the camera. My daughter Wendy was a ballerina, a beautiful little dancer. Now she's an actress," adds the proud papa.

Young had a role as a grandfather in the TV movie *Earth Angel* (1991). In this charming film a ghost from the sixties comes back to haunt a teenage girl in the nineties. Young plays the nineties girl's grandfather, and there's a wonderful scene where Grandpa is shown eating peanuts and watching *Mr. Ed!*

In 1989 Young played the somewhat naïve, bumbling neighbor, complete with plaid pants, on the short-lived CBS series *Coming of Age*. "I loved working on that show," says Alan. "I loved the people I worked with. They were just adorable. In my career, I've never worked with anybody I didn't like anyway." No doubt the feeling is mutual.

Bibliography

Bellamy, Ralph. *When the Smoke Hit the Fan.* Garden City, N.Y.: Doubleday, 1979.

Brooks, Tim. *The Complete Directory to Prime Time TV Stars.* New York: Ballantine, 1987.

_____, and Marsh, Earle. *The Complete Directory to Prime Time Network TV Shows, 1946–Present.* 4th ed. New York: Ballantine, 1988.

Burns, George, and Fisher, David. *All My Best Friends.* New York: G.P. Putnam's Sons, 1989.

Eisner, Joel, and Krinsky, David. *Television Comedy Series: An Episode Guide to 153 TV Sitcoms in Syndication.* Jefferson, N.C.: McFarland, 1984.

Holston, Kim. *Starlet: Biographies, Filmographies, TV Credits and Photos of 54 Famous and Not So Famous Leading Ladies of the Sixties.* Jefferson, N.C.: McFarland, 1988.

Katz, Ephraim. *The Film Encyclopedia.* New York: Putnam, 1979.

Katz, Susan. *Where Have They Gone?* New York: Grosset & Dunlap, 1980.

Lamparski, Richard. *Whatever Became of. . .?* 9th Series. New York: Crown, 1985.

_____. *Whatever Became of. . .?* 11th Series. New York: Crown, 1989.

Maltin, Leonard. *Leonard Maltin's TV Movies and Video Guide, 1991 Edition.* New York: Penguin, 1990.

Mitz, Rick. *The Great TV Sitcom Book.* New York: St. Martin's, 1980.

Russell, Jane. *My Path and My Detours.* New York: Watts, 1985.

Smith, Ronald L. *Sweethearts of Sixties TV.* New York: St. Martin's, 1989.

Weissman, Ginny, and Sanders, Coyne Steven. *The Dick Van Dyke Show: Anatomy of a Classic.* New York: St. Martin's, 1983.

Zicree, Marc Scott. *The Twilight Zone Companion.* New York: Bantam, 1982.

Index

Page numbers in **boldface** refer to photographs.

211

Index